THEATRICAL IMPRESSIONS

THEATRICAL IMPRESSIONS

BY
JULES LEMAÎTRE

Selected and Translated by Frederic Whyte

KENNIKAT PRESS
Port Washington, N. Y./London

THEATRICAL IMPRESSIONS

First published in 1924
Reissued in 1970 by Kennikat Press
Library of Congress Catalog Card No: 75-102847
SBN 8046-0757-5

Manufactured by Taylor Publishing Company   Dallas, Texas

CONTENTS

CONTENTS

INTRODUCTORY

THE name of Jules Lemaître is not yet familiar in this country, although some of his books have been translated and although M. Anatole France has sung his praises in an essay which must have been widely read. The *Impressions de Theâtre* are almost unknown to English readers. One curious indication of this will, perhaps, suffice. The London Library, which may fairly be taken to represent the class most interested in *belles lettres*, has had the first ten volumes of the series upon its shelves for more than a quarter of a century. Until quite recently many of the best pages in them were uncut.

And yet these delightful chronicles, with their almost unique blend of learned commentary, unconventional criticism and frank ingratiating self-revelation, ought surely to give wide pleasure. They should appeal, in the first place, to all lovers of things theatrical and things French ; secondly, to all lovers of Lemaître's chief masters,

7

Montaigne and Renan ; finally, to all lovers of good humour and naturalness and fun. If you can read the *Impressions* comfortably in the original, and have time for all the eleven volumes, by all means do so. If not, here is a selection, *faute de mieux*.

Translations are never satisfactory things, of course ; see Lemaître's own remarks upon the subject on page 262. And these *Impressions* are extraordinarily difficult to translate—perhaps more difficult even than the chiselled prose of Flaubert ; they are so essentially " impressions " rather than solemnly-ordered, meticulously-worded essays. In the French they are often as light as thistledown ; often, too, they are " thrown out for apprehension, not dissection," and translating is apt, sometimes, to be like dissecting. To certain fastidious Lemaîtrists, I fear, the pages which follow will seem lamentably inadequate, but they have been put together with ardour and delight, and I hope and trust that, for all their imperfections, they may serve their purpose and thus win new friends for one of the most admirable and lovable of Frenchmen.

" You can pick anywhere in Lemaître," a fellow-enthusiast wrote to me on learning of my

INTRODUCTORY

project, and when I started out upon it I myself felt inclined to this opinion. In practice, however, I very soon discovered it to be a mistaken one. For one reason or another, many of the things to which my impulse took me first and in fullest confidence turned out to be ineligible. It had seemed only right and proper, for instance, to begin with something about Corneille and Molière, and although Racine has, hitherto, meant little to us, recent writings by Mr. Lytton Strachey and Mr. Maurice Baring have stimulated our interest in that French idol, and therefore something about him, also, seemed desirable ; when dealing with these masters, however, Jules Lemaître is too obviously addressing himself to readers steeped in his own lore or, at least, to life-long frequenters of the Comédie Française. And then, the Greeks—one felt that it would be pleasant to present this ingenious and most suggestive Parisian mind upon the drama of Athens : I have had to content myself with one example. In the case of the modern French stage the chief trouble was, rather, the *embarras des richesses*, but I could not " pick anywhere " even in this field. Some of the *impressions* which probably meant most to the audience for whom they were written seemed to me too full of local and topical allusions for reproduction now and here. . . . I shall not weary the reader by dwelling further upon my difficulties. My selection must speak for itself.

THEATRICAL IMPRESSIONS

I

PORTE-SAINT-MARTIN : *Jeanne d'Arc*, a Drama-Legend in verse, in five Acts and six Scenes. By Jules Barbier.

UNKIND people keep complaining that I indulge in what they call "personal criticism." If I do so, it is from scruples of conscience. This week, for instance, when I have to tell how I witnessed a play dealing with Joan of Arc, am I not bound to explain that I went to it in a condition of mind which deprived me of any sort of freedom of judgment ? For so it is : in a work of this description, the parts which merely reproduce the legend (well or ill, it matters little) must always touch me to the depths of my soul, while those which are added by the author, whatever their merit, have on me the effect of tiresome bunglings, mere human interpolations in a Divine text. . . . That was the spirit in which I witnessed the Gospel as " adapted " recently by M. Busnach.

The story of Joan of Arc came to me, in truth, simultaneously with the Gospel—or was it a little earlier ?—and as a thing of the same order, as mysterious and as holy. I had spent the first years of my childhood in a *faubourg* of Orleans. The first verses which I had learnt by heart were not from the fables of La Fontaine or of Florian, they were the inferior verses (though to me they seemed so beautiful) written by Casimir Delavigne on the death of Joan of Arc. My earliest impressions of Art were those I derived from the second-rate equestrian statue of Joan in the Place du Martroi, Princess Marie's pious Joan in the Courtyard of the Hôtel de Ville, the passionate Joan in the Place des Tournelles. The first time my eyes were ever dazzled was by the procession of the 8th of May, a procession five miles long, if you please !—a Homeric *cortège* of all the parishes, of all the bodies corporate, of all the Societies of Mutual Support, from the entire region ; of all, indeed, who had any pretext whatever for donning a uniform, from the Clergy

to the Custom-House Officers, from the Red
Robes of the Court of Appeal to the Bousigny-de-
Canards band resplendent in their gold lace. And
the banners and the streamers! It was something like a Procession! And it grew in length
every year, until at last its head would be re-
entering the Cathedral while its tail was still
preparing to issue forth. . . .

And now for the first dramatic performance
at which I ever assisted. I was then three or
four years old, and never, never shall I again
experience a similar emotion. Through all the
years that I have been practising the strange
profession of critic of the theatre I have been
unable to recapture that rapture. Neither the
fresh sincerity of Émile Augier, nor the mystical
fierceness of Dumas *fils*, nor the red and white
magic of Sardou, nor even the delicious irony
of Meilhac can give it back to me; for all of
them together cannot give me back my short
breeches or my ignorance or the astonishment
of my eyes as they made the discovery of
life.

It was in the Cirque Franconi, during the Fair
on the Mall. An *équestrienne*, who seemed to me
infinitely lovely, made her appearance standing
on the saddle of a white horse, a saddle as wide

as a terrace. This woman was all the more impressive in that she wore five or six costumes, super-imposed. And while the big white horse went round and round on the track, she was first of all the shepherdess who heard the Voices beneath the Fairies' Tree. She then discarded her russet gown and shepherd's crook. Now she was the Warrior-Maiden, brandishing her sword— the innocent sword which leads on but kills not, and which is nothing but a crucifix reversed. Next, removing her cuirass and casting the sword aside (a stableman doubtless picked up these accessories, but him I did not see) she seemed to rise aloft—the Consecration of Rheims was now in progress—all in white and holding up high and straight the White Banner embroidered in *fleurs-de-lys*. And I, who knew that these were the flowers of France and the flowers of our Kings, whose pictures I had seen in a child's history-book (among them, that of King Pharamond, " who, perhaps, never existed ") rejoiced in my scarce-burgeoning heart and felt vaguely proud to know that I, tiny boy that I was, in my fourth year, had behind me so many centuries of glory and suffering and fortitude. . . . But now the *équestrienne* doffed her triumphal trappings, and it was only a poor prisoner in rags we saw, carrying upon her delicate wrists a long chain, which swung from side to side like a garland. At this, I could restrain myself no longer, my nose puckered up and I wept bitterly. Finally, the fair lady, now slighter than ever, appeared in the garb of a martyr, in a white dress, girdled with a cord, her eyes raised to Heaven, pressing to her breast a small wooden cross, her hair loose and flowing out behind her like a banner in the red apotheosis of Bengal light, to the rhythmical galloping of the white horse, going round and round and round. . . . I would have liked it to continue for ever and ever. . . .

That, assuredly, was the most beautiful poem on Joan of Arc that I have ever seen.

There is within the heart of every one of us (at least, I like to think so) a secret hoard of inherited instincts, feelings and beliefs, against which the critics are powerless, and which, more-over, we ourselves will not suffer to be touched ; for, to begin with, it would be vain to try to touch them, for we keep them in the marrow of our bones ; and then, supposing we could rid ourselves of them, we know well what we should lose but not what there might be for us to gain.

THEATRICAL IMPRESSIONS

. . . The love, the worship, the veneration of Joan of Arc is for me one of these feelings. I came to know the Passion of Joan at the same time as the Passion of Christ, and the one seemed to me almost like a French version of the other. It is the most beautiful story of heroism, of self-sacrifice, of unselfishness, of converse with a higher world. Dreams? What matters that, since dreams are the very condition and instrument of the moral progress of this world? This story of the Maid is as amazing, as romantic, as far removed from the ordinary course of life, as that of Alexander or Napoleon, and it has more of beauty in it. It is one of those stories which seem most clearly to bear witness to something like a Divine intervention amid the darkness and chaos of fatally-linked events that lead us we know not whither—most clearly, also, to prove that it is not impossible that this world (and I mean by this world the infinitesimal corner of the universe in which we live and of which we can form a conception) may have a meaning, a *raison d'être*, a purpose. I realised this much more clearly thirty years ago than I do now. Then, in truth, I did understand Joan. And her story moved me all the more because I saw in her a sister to all small children, to the humble and to the poor

—saw that she was only a peasant just as I myself was a little peasant and could understand all she said, and that she had done great things without being a great lady or a great scholar, and just by believing and loving. In my eyes she was like another Blessed Virgin, but standing closer to me, more active, more conceivable, more exciting to my small boy's mind.

Through her I came to understand what the national divinities could be to the ancients when they had pious minds. Soon I had my heart full of her legend and her cult : like an Athenian brought up in the love of Pallas-Athene. Is she not called the Maid, just like Pallas ? For she has the crowning charm of purity. And we adore purity—even if we are wanting in the practice of it—because impurity seems to us the greatest enemy of beneficent and unselfish action, because we feel the terrible egoism of carnal loves, even of those which are excusable for their very recklessness and for the pain that follows in their wake, and because, finally, it is by not giving one's body to anyone that one can give one's soul to all, and because purity seems to us one of the conditions and even one of the forms of universal charity . . . And thus when I think

B

of Joan of Arc, I see her as Dante Rossetti saw
" the blessed Damosel " :

> " La demoiselle bénie se penchait en dehors,
> Appuyée sur la barrière dorée du ciel ;
> Ses yeux étaient plus profonds que l'abîme
> Des eaux apaisées, au soir ;
> Elle avait trois lis à la main,
> Et sept étoiles dans les cheveux. . . ."*

*　　　*　　　*

I am sorry that M. Jules Barbier's verse is not
always as beautiful as it needed to be. I admit
also that the additions he has thought it necessary
to make, in order to give the aspect of a drama
to this mystery (the scenes of the King, of Iseult
and Lahire, those of the soldiers and their leaders
before Orleans), seemed to me too long and left
me cold. But all those parts which reproduced
the best known features of the legend remain
(in spite of the great boobies of Alexandrines)
sublime and exquisite in themselves. There were
moments in which this wretched cold-blooded
" First-Night " Paris knew a thrill. . . . How to
account for that ? Talking the other day of a
tragedy performed at the Odéon, I said (and

* It seems better to give here the French version tran-
scribed by Jules Lemaître rather than the original lines.

why should I try to say it now in other words ?
I might say it even worse) :

" At such moments one yields, one mocks no
more. 'A spirit,' said Job, ' passed before my
face ; the hair of my flesh stood up.' What
has come to us ? One of those emotions, one
of those rare, strange movements of the soul that
make a man come out of himself and forget
himself—forget his own troubles and his private
interests and, in a sort of ecstasy akin to madness, act against his own nature and aim at a
goal which is beyond him and a good in which
he personally will have no share : one of those
inexplicable emotions to which we owe all the
great deeds in the history of mankind, and by
means of which, in truth, mankind endures and
is maintained, is expressed to us in words which
bring us into communion with it, which plunge
it deep into our hearts—doubtless because the
poet first experienced it himself with a peculiar
intensity. It may be compared to an internal
flash of lightning which strikes and blinds us."

Some flashes of this kind leap forth from M.
Jules Barbier's tragedy, thanks, perhaps, to Mme.
Sarah Bernhardt. Despite the artificiality of a
diction too persistently rhythmical and an en-
feebled voice which was not equal to the great

cries it has to utter, she was admirable, first in the child-like state of trance (like the Joan of Bastien-Lepage), then impelled by sheer exaltation (Jeanne de Fremiet's Joan, this), next in the phase of poignant, naïve misery, and finally in that of supernatural serenity (such a Joan as Gustave Moreau could paint if he would) : and all this with the somewhat hieratic harmony of attitudes which seem to make a figure fade into the legendary past. Beforehand, it had vexed me that Mme. Sarah Bernhardt should play the rôle of the Maid. I should be very sorry now if she had not played it There is a potency in this woman.

[1890   Vol. V.]*

* For the convenience of the reader who may like to read these *Impressions* in the original I give references to the volumes of the French edition in which they appear. Jules Lemaître began writing them towards the end of 1885. They appeared as *feuilletons* in the *Journal des Débats.*—F. W.

II

Comédie Française : *Les Petits Oiseaux,* a
Comedy in three Acts by Eugène Labiche.

I DID not succeed altogether in rediscovering
in *Les Petits Oiseaux* the outstanding
merits I thought I saw in the play fifteen
years ago.

It must be admitted that fifteen years ago I
was even more the prey than I am now of all
sorts of influences and prejudices. I had not
then sworn an oath unto myself to devote all
my energies and all my thoughts to liking only
what pleased me and to liking everything that
pleased me : a purpose which was full of pride
and presumption, and which I shall doubtless
not realise, if I realise it at all, until my old
age—if I have an old age. And it will be too
late then to reap the fruit of a state of mind
attained so tardily.

Now, in those days, I knew that one had to
like and admire Labiche, and I made no

difficulties about it whatever. On the contrary. Émile Augier had just edited the dramatic works of his friend, with a Preface in which he declared Labiche to be great and attributed genius to him. We had had, moreover, a long period during which no one had ventured to be gay, and the gaiety of Labiche had the aspect, therefore, of something new, something that had come back to us, and we were grateful to him. This gaiety of his was pre-eminently Gallic ; it presented a national character and thus inspired a sort of consideration and respect at a moment when we were all full of ideas about reconstituting the forces of the nation. And it was a wholesome kind of gaiety. Labiche being, to a really astonishing degree, ignorant of women, or else disdainful of them, some of his best vaudevilles seemed almost like extravagant caricatures, wildly contemptuous parodies, of the dramas of passion and adultery to which we were used ; whereas MM. Meilhac and Halévy, without actually inculcating bad morals, were introducing a touch of piquancy and prettiness into their pictures of immorality, and representing it all too often as bound up with sweetness and kindliness and a certain lovable softness of disposition. Finally, it had become the vogue to speak of the

LABICHE

" lyrical " quality of Labiche's writing—there was talk also about the " bitterness " and " depth " to be observed in them ; and, with a pleasing consciousness of saying something a little paradoxical, we would make out this good-humoured vaudevillist to be the equal of the three or four greatest dramatic authors of the century. In short, Labiche was all the fashion. He was the first vaudevillist, pure and simple, to be elected a member of the French Academy (and assuredly it was one of the most intelligent elections the Academy ever made). The most literary and critical and most distinguished *salons* contended for him. And, in common with the novels of Dumas *père*, Labiche's plays were commended to all convalescents and sufferers from gout.

I had found keen enjoyment, then, in the ten volumes of this great jester's farces, so easily and sympathetically put together and so full of natural light-heartedness. But I remember that I found a quite peculiar grace in *Les Petits Oiseaux*, and that even in the reading of the text I experienced a certain slight and delectable surprise. What was the explanation ? Merely that in the rest of Labiche's productions, which were marked more by abundance than variety, while I delighted in all those little portraits and silhouettes *à la* Paul de Kock and Monnier, reproduced by this inspired Merry-Andrew, I had been conscious that something lacked. Never had I met a woman in Labiche—no, not in a single play. For one cannot give the name of woman to such pale abstractions as the wives of the Perrichons and Champbourcys, or as their daughters, or as the very sketchy outlines of dissatisfied old maids or unfortunate little *cocottes* who turn up occasionally in his absurdities. Woman, in Labiche's plays, is reduced strictly to a " utility rôle." Strange to note, you do not meet in them even the feminine types you would expect a writer of such Gallic temperament to introduce : *commères de fabliau*, for instance, or ample, quick-tongued *bourgeoises*, or *maîtresses-servantes*, after the style of the Dorines and the Martons. No, not even any of these. Nothing. For this *solognot** of a Labiche woman might almost not have any existence !

Now there are, of course, no more women in *Les Petits Oiseaux* than in Labiche's other vaudevilles ; but we have in it, at least, Jeanne Aubertin's pretty little disquisition about the sparrows who are hungry and to whom crumbs

* Solognot = inhabitant of the region of the Sologne.

must be thrown ; and, above all, pervading the whole piece, there is a feeling of sweetness and kindness, almost of tenderness, of a sort one is almost tempted to call womanly, and forming a unique contrast with the hard joviality and rough buffoonery to which Labiche abandons himself completely in the rest of his work.

This it was, I think, that charmed me so much in *Les Petits Oiseaux* and that caused me to overlook its general weakness and faultiness. On seeing it again at the Comédie (on a stage too large for it, by the way), I felt quite differently. The truth is that the piece has no sense, or to speak more precisely (for how many very pretty attractive vaudevilles have no sense !), that it seems at first to have " a moral," that the author himself warns us that it has a moral, that we are on the look out for a moral all the time, and that the curtain falls without our having discovered it.

Here are the three phases through which the *bourgeois* M. Blandinet has to pass.

1° He is gentle, timid, confiding, credulous. He is good and believes absolutely in the goodness of others. He does not dare to raise his tenants' rents. He allows the bootmaker Mizabran, who owes him for five or six quarters, to make him, " on account " of rent, any number of pairs of boots which he will never wear. He is open-handed with his son and gives him all the money he wants. He has a quite young wife, whom he suffers to go and come as she pleases. He leaves the keys about in the rooms, having so much confidence in his servant Joseph. Finally, one of his old friends, a merchant named Aubertin, having need of 50,000 francs, Blandinet offers him the money and promises to let him have it next day. Suddenly . . .

2° Blandinet discovers that a fraudulent beggar has played a trick on him. Apparently it is the first time this *bourgeois* of fifty has discovered that there are men who lie and deceive, and it is the first time that he himself has been deceived. And instantly Blandinet becomes ferocious ; he who had believed everything, now will believe nothing. He resumes possession of all the keys. He becomes suspicious of Miza-bran, and discovers that this bootmaker has been passing cowhide off on him for calf. He has all the butcher's meat weighed. He counts the pieces of sugar in the sugar-bowl and observes, a quarter of an hour later, that three are missing ; therefore Joseph is a thief. He remarked that his wife, who went out to the baths two hours ago, has not yet come home : she is unfaithful to him. Finally, just as he is on the point of sending his friend Aubertin the promised 50,000 francs, he changes his mind and writes a letter of refusal.

3° Second change of outlook. Blandinet finds he is ruined by the flight of a banker. Now he is overwhelmed with kind actions. Aubertin, whose affairs have mended, comes, bringing him not only his 50,000 francs but a deed of partnership. His brother François, whom he thought hard and selfish, shows himself no less generous. His tenants, even the bootmaker Mizabran, bring him their arrears of rent. Joseph wants to go on serving him without wages. Blandinet discovers now that it was his nephew who took the three lumps of sugar, and that his wife had been back at home quite a long time when he was imagining her still away " at the baths." . . . And he exclaims : " *Mon Dieu !* *Mon Dieu !* How good everyone is ! "

What, I ask you, is one to make out of this story ? The author has woven a special kind of humanity round Blandinet, for Blandinet's own personal use. All the time he is suspecting and distrusting people, they are proving themselves marvels of thoughtfulness, unselfishness and devotion. What is he to believe ? He concludes that the apparent trickery of the bogus beggar must have been merely something accidental and exceptional and certainly of no importance. So he returns to his normal original self. He has learnt nothing ; his goodness of character remains unchanged ; or, rather, one has no more real knowledge than in the first Act as to whether it amounts to real goodness.

Supposing that at the moment when the curtain begins to fall Blandinet were to discover a second time that someone was deceiving him—what would happen ? Obviously the ideas which he cherishes regarding mankind would change once more and the piece would begin all over again.

And yet how very easy it would have been— how few modifications would have been required !—to arrange the story of Blandinet in such a fashion that a very charming and highly moral lesson might evolve from it and at the same time a pleasing definition of goodness.

First of all, as at present, Blandinet would be fool enough to see good everywhere and he would be roughly disabused of this illusion. Then, enraged, he would see evil everywhere. But, instead of his being now surrounded, as in Labiche, by persons of such exquisite feelings that he sinks back into his first mistake, I would have him

establish the fact that in some instances he had
divined matters aright and thus become hardened
in his pessimism.   Then, suddenly, a good action
should be revealed to him where he had scented a
piece of rascality, and he would thus have been
corrected in his second extreme, without returning
to his first.   His former goodness would be re-
gained, but it would be purified and fortified by
these two experiences ; he would regain it with
delight because he would have been very unhappy
while distrusting all the world.   And the moral of
the story would be that, after all, the chances of
being mistaken are about equal, whether you
believe in men or don't believe in them, but that
one loses more than one gains by distrusting men
altogether ; that, if one is always on one's guard,
one hasn't time to be good ; that one must begin
by being good, while remaining on one's guard a
little ; and, in short, that the best rule of life is
to believe that men are worth nothing and to
treat them, poor creatures, as though they were
worth something.   To be indulgent to all without
expecting anything from anybody—that is the
rule of life we come to by whatever route we
travel ; whether by the reflection that all men
have been redeemed by the same blood and that
God alone is the Judge of all hearts ; or, on the

contrary, by the thought that it does not do for us to be hard on each other, as we are all fellow sufferers, knowing nothing of our common origin or our common destiny : in short, whether we are influenced by religious zeal and faith or by a smiling and ironic passiveness with few convictions as to human responsibility—whether by Christian charity or by Epicureanism : two states of mind that, although radically different, come together often enough in their beneficent effects : the best states of mind, both of them, in which it is possible to be.

Despite all one can say in criticism of *Les Petits Oiseaux*, the play pleases by its air of sweetness and warmth of heart. It is a very merry *berquinade*, which, after all, is a somewhat rare combination. The episode of Blandinet's brother, François, which unfolds itself side by side with the principal action, is full of a rich humour that becomes mingled with tears towards the end. The Uncle François, a mill-owner from Elbeuf, is a terrible fellow, " a man of principle." The moment his son, Tiburce, has qualified for the law, his allowance is cut off, for " a young man must learn how to manage ' on his own.' " Whenever the son writes to tell his father that he can't get work and is dying of starvation, the latter remarks : " I know that story ! " Tiburce has made shift as best he could. He has been to the moneylenders. Naturally he has not been able to redeem his notes of hand, and at last, in desperation, he gets arrested on the Boulevards walking arm-in-arm with his father—we are still in the period of imprisonment for debt. His father is indignant. There is a sharp fire of questions. " What did you mean by signing these things ? " " I was starving ! " " You should have written to me." " I did write to you and you replied : ' I know that story ! ' " The " man of principle " holds out no longer ; the father's heart softens within the breast of the man of business. He looks tenderly at Tiburce and perceives that the boy looks pale and ill ; he feels his son's arms. " Poor thin little arms ! " . . . No need to describe to you the softening of the hard François which now takes place, simultaneously with the hardening of the soft Blandinet. One has been looking forward to this change-about upon parallel lines and in contrary directions, and that always produces pleasure.

[4th August, 1890. Vol. VI.]

III

COMÉDIE FRANÇAISE : Revival of *Le Demi-Monde*, a Comedy in five Acts by Alexandre Dumas *fils*.

A PERIOD of disfavour awaits all master-pieces—all those, at least, in which the observation of manners that are to some degree transitory holds a certain place. This period seems to be reached at the end of thirty or forty years. *Le Demi-Monde* belongs to 1855. It suffers now from depicting a world which is no longer quite close to us but which is not yet far enough away. We have the feeling : " It is still like that to-day, and yet not quite like that." Baronne d'Ange, Mme. de Vernières, Mme. de Santis, do still exist, but their dresses are not the same fashion—or the same price ; nor do they talk or amuse themselves in quite the same way, nor have they quite the same kind of trinkets about them. Moreover, they do not form quite so distinct a group as they did ; the " half-world," as defined by the author, is now

C

much more mingled with the world at large ; it is no longer " a floating island adrift upon the ocean of Parisian life " : the island has been all but merged in the continent.

That is why the work, in places, seems to " date," like the best comedies of Augier—and as Molière, no doubt, " dated " under the Regency. But M. Dumas showed in his *Avant-Propos* that he was prepared for this and we must not reproach him for what was inevitable. When the forms of fashionable libertinism shall have become still more different from what they were in 1855, in thirty years from now, perhaps—and quite certainly a century hence—the work will date no longer : it will be an antique, which is a very different thing.

One feels that this will be the fate of *Le Demi-Monde*, that it will retain its flavour, for it is full of all kinds of things, true things and human things ; and, throughout almost the whole of it, its style is strong and firm. I witnessed, with an interest which never flagged, this revival of the piece ; then I re-read it, and it seemed to me even better to read than to see. And this bodes well for it.

It is, as I have said, extremely rich in matter. It is one of those works about which " one can

talk." To-day I shall discuss only the " case "
of Olivier de Jalin. I ask myself these two
questions : Is Olivier's action justifiable ? If it
is, why does Olivier inspire in me so hesitant a
sense of sympathy ?

Our present-day morals must be in a queer
condition for it to seem to me necessary to raise
the first of these two questions, and for it to be
possible that anyone should dispute Olivier's
right to prevent the marriage between the clever,
scheming courtesan and his honest and candid
friend, Raymond de Nanjac. It is to be noted
that all that can be urged against Olivier has been
expressed by the author himself, through the
mouth of Suzanne, the courtesan in question, with
more force and clearness and eloquence than it has
been by anyone else. The passage deserves to be
cited in full ; all the more, because people always
pretend to forget it :

" By what right have you acted as you have
done ? What have you against me ? If M. de
Nanjac were an old friend of yours, if you and he
had been brought up together or if you were
brothers, it would be different, but no, you have
only known him a week or two. If you had no
personal motive—but are you certain you haven't
been prompted by wounded vanity ? You don't

care for me—I know that ; but one is always a little sore when a person whom one supposed to care for one declares that that is all over. It comes to this, that because you took it into your head to make love to me and because I was simple enough to trust you and think you a man of honour—because I did, perhaps, love you—you are now making yourself into an obstacle to my life's happiness. Have I compromised you ? Have I ruined you ? Was I even unfaithful to you ? Even granting that I am not morally fit for the name and position it is my ambition to achieve—and of course that *must* be granted, because it is true—is it for you, who helped to make me unfit, to close against me the honourable road I want to follow ? No, my dear Olivier, that is not fair. When one has had a share in a person's weaknesses, it isn't right to take sides against her. A man who has had a woman's love—no matter in what degree—if there has been nothing base and calculating in that love, is in her debt always, *always* ; and whatever he may do to serve her, he will never make up to her for what she has given him." (Act III, Scene XI.)

To think of all Olivier could say in reply ! . . . He says only, " In my place, there isn't a man of

36

honour who wouldn't have done as I have done " ;
adding, " For Raymond's sake, I was right to
speak ; *for your sake, I ought to have kept silence.*"
Just at this moment, he is obliged—or imagines
he is obliged—to be wary.

But how delighted I should be to hear him say :
" For heaven's sake don't let us muddle our
brains by going into the relative importance of
duties. . . . In making the claims you do, you
are trying to turn to an unfair use the sentiment
that prompts a man of gentlemanly instincts to
treat his companion of pleasure as he would treat
a woman he really loved—a mistress in the real
sense of the word—simulating a respect for her
which he does not feel and pretending to be grateful to her for favours which he has already paid
for in one way or another. And in order to act
up to this code of behaviour you wish me to
renounce an imperative duty—the duty of
protecting an innocent person from misfortune,
from lifelong misfortune ; and that person my
friend, a friend who has asked me to speak the
truth to him and to save him if he is in danger.
You say I have no obligation towards M. de
Nanjac. What, I ask you, is my obligation
towards you ? When we met, we came to terms,
as you know well. I counted on getting some

pleasure out of you ; I don't know whether you counted on getting any pleasure out of me—why not ?—but at all events, in view of my character and my position in the world, you thought that our affair together would be a satisfactory experience, and that is why you didn't ask to be paid anything. You admit that my conduct would be all right if Nanjac were an old friend of mine, if we had known each other all our lives. Well, but how if, after knowing him for only a fortnight, I have as much regard and esteem for him as though I had known him thirty years ? Such things have happened. Anyway I have enough regard for him to feel bound to save him if I can. You say that I can do this only by wronging and sacrificing you. I am not wronging you by trying to prevent you from doing something evil. I am not damaging your position or your livelihood. You have nothing to complain of, with the handsome allowance M. de Thonnerins has settled on you in return for your having been his mistress. In forcing you to abandon this marriage, I leave you just as you stood before. I don't take anything from you ; I merely prevent you from achieving what you could not achieve without lying and treachery and crime. For Nanjac believes you to be a widow

38

and you are not, because you have never married.
He believes you are Baronne d'Ange, and you are
not. He thinks you have never had any lovers,
and you have had lovers. He thinks your money
has come to you from your family, and it comes
from an old lover. If Nanjac marries you, he
will be regarded as the most dishonoured of men
and he will be all the more miserable if he discovers your treachery. If, indeed, he had not
questioned me, I might have had some excuse for
allowing the evil to take place. But he appealed
to my loyalty ; to deceive him would have been
to make myself an accomplice in your crime. I
wish, indeed, that my trifling indebtedness to you
were compatible with the duty, the infinitely
important duty, which I feel I owe to him, but it
is not. There is no room for hesitation. Confess all to Nanjac and, if he can overlook it, I
won't say I shall rejoice for his sake, but at least
I shall do nothing against you. If you won't
speak, however, I must. Call me a blackguard
if you like. I must put up with that. . . . I
should be doing what I am doing even if you had
really cared for me. Only in that case I should
be feeling much more distressed and what I
should regard as my duty to you would weigh
much more evenly in the scales with my duty

to my friend. But you admit that those love-letters you sent me were written for you by Mme. de Santis and that you did not even read them. You are altogether too clever, Suzanne, and, apart from everything else, that alone is enough to simplify the matter."

Such are the things Olivier should say—in the style of M. Dumas, which would be more effective. In short, I give my full and unreserved approval to Olivier's conduct, and yet Olivier's personality does not appeal to me, and though I commend him I cannot quite like him.* Why? This

---

* Dumas, in a vehement reply to other critics of his comedy, declared that Olivier de Jalin was " *le plus honnête homme* " of his acquaintance. One can understand Dumas, but it is difficult to understand how Jules Lemaître could have felt any sympathy for Olivier at all. Perhaps some of those other critics had aroused a controversial spirit in him by extravagant pleas for Suzanne ? One would have expected Lemaître to take a view similar to that which Henry James expressed (in " Portraits of Places ") some years earlier. Mme d'Ange impressed Henry James as " a superior woman "—the whole interest of the play, to him, was " in her being a superior woman." " Olivier has been her lover ; he himself is one of the reasons why she may not marry Nanjac ; he has given her a push along the downward path. But it is curious how little this is held by the author to disqualify him from fighting the battle in which she is so much the weaker combatant." An English audience, Henry James went on to declare, would have expressed its feelings in some such words as : " I say, that's not fair game. Can't you leave the woman alone ! " Usually it is the French who are entitled to call the English Pharisees, but here the position is very surprisingly reversed.—F. W.

brings me to my " Secondly," as they say in sermons.

The fact is that Olivier lacks humility—even modesty. He is aggressive in his self-righteousness. He is too clever and self-complacent. He does his duty, a difficult and trying, and somewhat cruel duty, without looking into his own heart. This *honnête homme*, called upon to serve the ends of justice and to act in the name of verities in which he surely must firmly believe and by which his whole soul must be penetrated, this " man of goodwill " would seem to have no inner life. Or if he has, we are not allowed to realise it. The only sign he gives of it is that, having set out to seduce a married woman (Mme. de Lornans), he pulls up short, restrained by a scruple. But even in regard to this he seems a little too much pleased with himself. Beyond a doubt he is morally the superior of Suzanne, but he is too conscious of it—too soon, and too unconcernedly. The more his conduct in regard to Suzanne proves his faith in a moral verity, the more concerned he should show himself as to his own virtue, which hitherto has been all too " latent " and too scantily fertile in virtuous acts. I would gladly see him stand up against Suzanne in a more downright fashion than he does, with less circumlocution and diplomacy, but with more modesty and gentleness and indulgence in his words. I would like his whole attitude to express this idea : " If I am opposing you, if I am barring the way to you, it is on the strength of a duty clear as day—a duty which I cannot shirk without proving myself a scoundrel ; I am doing it, not, alas, on the strength of my past life, which is far from beautiful. I am an instrument of justice to-day because I *have* to be ; because, after all, I am a man not without honour ; but I am conscious of my own unworthiness and I know that this present action of mine is better than I am myself."

For you must remember what kind of man this Olivier de Jalin really is : a *viveur*, a typical *boulevardier*, a votary of pleasure. The kind of life which he now castigates in his talk is the life he has always lived, and deliberately lived. In the first Act he makes some confidences to Mme. de Vernières : " . . . And that, my dear Comtesse, is how it has come about that I was left to my own devices so young and that I committed follies and raised debts." At another moment we hear him saying to Hippolyte Richond : " If I have lived too fast a life, I am at least *un honnête* *homme** and I am resolved to commit no more of those little infamies of which love is the pretext. To go to a man's house, to clasp his hand, to call him your friend, and to take his wife from him— well, if others think differently, so much the worse for them !—but to me that has become shameful, repugnant, sickening." As he undertakes not to do such things any more it is clear he has done them in the past.

And, in truth, Olivier de Jalin has until this moment led the life of an idler and a debauchee. He has spent the previous fifteen years or so amusing himself—eating, drinking, gambling, playing about with young women of easy virtue, and, between whiles, leading astray the wives of his friends. I know, of course, that in the theatre it is an understood thing that all this is nothing ; that *viveurs* are invariably there represented as sympathetic personalities and that it is always supposed that the brutal kind of existence they have lived has somehow developed in them an extreme generosity combined with an extraordinary delicacy of feeling. All the *mauvais sujets* of the stage have hearts of gold and in

* As Dumas uses this expression so pointedly in the play, and as an exact English equivalent is lacking, I leave it untranslated.—F. W.

questions of money especially display an incorruptible honesty. Look at the Marquis de Presles, the Duc d'Aléria, Champrosay in the *Famille Benoiton*, and how many others ! But to my mind that is one of the falsest and most pernicious—I am tempted to add also one of the most inept and dishonest—conventions of which the stage is guilty. In the world about me I have never observed that the *viveurs*, the pleasure-seeking idlers, have had such beautiful natures, nor has it struck me that debauchery, gambling and dependence upon moneylenders in one's early or later youth have necessarily resulted at a maturer age in an unusual endowment of integrity and kindliness ; what I have noticed is that many of the men of this order have, when come to ruin, married rich wives, while the best ones among them continue to be amiable sots and the worst become appalling Pharisees. . . .

Olivier, for his part, declines to become a Pharisee of the fashionable worldly type—there are Pharisees of many types. He has escaped the demoralisation which generally results from the unbridled pursuit of a life of pleasure : my compliments to him upon that ! But in his struggle with Suzanne he ought to remember that he has been very much as she is : throughout a long period he has sought pleasure, and the same kind of pleasure, in just the same way as she has.

Suzanne, no doubt, sought money as well, but it is more than probable that a woman of her intelligence and pride would not have been content with mere pleasure had she been as rich as Olivier. . . . Then, at a certain moment, the soul of the worldling cannot have differed much from the soul of the light-of-love ; or, at least, both have seemed to assign the same purpose to their lives. And finally, he has been her lover ; they have made acquaintance together with the husks of swine : that is a bond. She has seen him in a certain light and in certain attitudes. He has played with her the comedy of love and, doubtless, in the intervals, the comedy of respect. He has said to her certain words which were not true. And, while assuredly, those words should not prevent him to-day from acting as he does (for he is obeying a duty which comes before all else), at least he should regret profoundly having uttered them : and that is what I should like to feel in his actions and in his words. I should like him to combat his former companion in vice with resolution but without bitterness or pride, rather with sadness, deep grief, and with a persistent sense of humiliation. I should like him to say to her : " I feel that I cannot perform this good action without asking pardon of the great courage I reveal in doing so as a man unworthy by reason of his past to exhibit so much virtue now ; and this false and lamentable bearing of mine in achieving what is good—this is my chastisement."

Instead of that, Olivier is sparkling and brilliant and discharges witticisms and aphorisms all around him like fireworks. He appears proud and hard, he has maintained his worldly sharpness and assurance, he shows himself a man of force and address. His conduct, I repeat, is absolutely legitimate ; but he has not acquired a state of mind in keeping with his conduct. This it is that irks me a little, as well as the idea that the author is not altogether of my mind as to Olivier's moral worth in the past, and even a little in the present : for if the things Olivier does are spoilt for me by the way he does them, it is obvious that they are not so spoilt for M. Dumas. On the contrary. But for my part, I admit, I would give all the witticisms of Olivier for a little hint of gentleness and humility here and there. Oh, how refreshing that would be.

DUMAS FILS

Need I repeat now that *Le Demi-Monde* is, none the less, a very fine play, that the drama enacted by Suzanne and Nanjac is singularly moving, and that the rôle of Suzanne d'Ange is from start to finish admirable in its truth ?

[8th April, 1890.   Vol. V.]

IV

Gymnase : *Froufrou*, a Play in 5 Acts by MM. Meilhac et Halévy.

THE Gymnase has revived *Froufrou* ; it could not have given me a greater pleasure. *Froufrou* is MM. Meilhac et Halévy's one " serious " comedy and the one comedy they have written with a tragic ending. It retains the piquant grace of their dramatic fantasies and, in addition, it has tears in it and deep and penetrating emotion. It is a moving drama which is at the same time a ravishing comedy of manners ; among moving dramas it is, I think, the simplest. It is a story all of one piece, unfolding itself with incomparable smoothness and clarity—with nothing in it of that sense of straining and effort which one is conscious of sometimes in the plays of Augier and Dumas, two men of power in whom grace lacks a little.

It is to be remarked, indeed, that except in just three or four of their deliberate imbroglios, the outstanding characteristic of the work of Meilhac and Halévy is absolute simplicity of conception, composition and style—I am almost tempted to call it Attic simplicity. Over and above this, their plays are full of the most acute, and least pedantic, kind of observation, wholly unpretentious, without forced witticisms, and yet with wit pervading the whole dialogue ; and, then, their divine gift of fancy, of capricious imagination, side by side with the precise observation, and the still rarer gift of modernity—of that intangible attribute in a play or in a novel which makes us feel we are having shown us the very latest aspect of our habits and modes of life ; and finally, with all this wit and caprice and irony (one is at a loss to say how), a touch of tenderness, here and there (as in *la Petite Mère* and in *la Cigale*)—a gift of human sympathy and compassion. All these faculties, lifted up just for once from mere vaudeville to a higher plane, were to combine to produce *Froufrou*, the least ambitious, the easiest and the most charming of our *grandes comédies*.

The heroine is adorable, and how living she is ! She is, indeed, a woman of this *fin de siècle*, but a woman captured, so to speak, in process of formation before she has become incurably unfeeling and wrong-headed. Since we saw her first, we have seen Paulette, who is almost devoid of heart and feeling, who, indeed, has almost nothing in her but curiosity. Froufrou is woman enough to be able to love and to suffer. But until the moment when she dies of what there is of goodness in her birdlike nature, she is a deliciously frivolous little animal, avid of action and excitement, with emotions so swift and so changing that one may ask oneself whether she has within her any conscience or sense of morality at all: yet she is exquisite, and we adore her for her beauty, her vivacity, her frailty, her futility. These little creatures fascinate us by the very mystery of their emptiness, and by the dizzying speed of their perpetual movement. They have a disturbing enchantment in them ; there is something almost painful in the impossibility of seizing them, fixing them, holding them. One loves them with a forlorn love. . . .

" Frailty, irresponsibility, capriciousness, thy name is woman ! "—that is true ; but if you say : " Woman, thy name is gentleness, devotion, sacrifice ! "—that is true also ; and we have, side by side with Froufrou, the sweet Louise, her sister, all graciousness and serene goodness in her plain head-band and black dress—Louise, the resigned, to whom involuntarily I give the gentle, modest and pure profile of Hippolyte

THEATRICAL IMPRESSIONS

Flandrin's *Jeune Fille*—you know the picture, it is in the Louvre. As between Louise and Froufrou Sartorys never hesitates. As he is a man of serious mind and somewhat preoccupied, it is naturally the wild and giddy-headed sister whom he chooses, not suspecting that Louise loves him and that Louise would mean his happiness. . . . From this moment onwards, note how easily and logically the drama unfolds itself. Froufrou spends her time dressing and chattering and sparkling and froufrou-ting. She and her lovable father, most modern and least sober-minded of parents, amuse themselves play-acting, and as she does not trouble herself about her home or her child or her husband, the good Louise, summoned by Froufrou herself, instals herself by the hearth-side and slowly, gently, without wishing or intending to do so, takes her place. Meanwhile, what was bound to happen, happens. Froufrou is tempted ; she thinks she loves M. de Valréas ; she becomes a prey to fear ; she would fain change her method of life and reclaim the place she has abandoned to her sister. But her husband refuses to take her seriously and treats her like a young girl—or like a mistress. Who, then, is to save her ? Her father ? He is too frivolous, he does not understand or he is afraid of understanding. Her son ? He is with Tante Louise. Louise has taken everything from her, both son and husband. Ah, she reflects, so that is how things are ! No one will help her ! Very well, she will follow the line along which she is being forced ! And it is in this kind of mood of desperation that the linnet-like Froufrou goes to her doom. . . . Poor Froufrou ! What a miracle that third act is ! What perfect and delicate observation there is in the scenes between Froufrou and her husband and her father and between the two sisters ! What life and what truth in the dialogue ! How easily and naturally the whole course of the play, down to the frenzied flight of the poor desperate little being ! I do not know whether in the whole of the contemporary drama there is anything so strong and so supple in its strength.

Now, we find her with Valréas at Venice in the city of gondolas and of romance. The outlook is all gloom for the luckless lovers, they are bored to death and have to make desperate efforts to persuade themselves that they suffice to each other. " Are you happy ? " Mme. de Cambri asks Froufrou. " Oh, yes ! " she replies. " What would become of me if I were not happy ! " Her husband, Sartorys, arrives—he comes to return Froufrou her *dot*, which she has refused to take back. He kills Valréas. Sartorys shows himself very hard. That he should kill Valréas is quite all right, but he ought to understand, and feel some pity for, this poor Froufrou. Pity should come *sooner* to him, that is to say. . . . Froufrou goes to her father's, but she is very ill.

. . One day she makes her way to her husband's, a supplicant ; she sees her boy again and dies forgiven. *We* had forgiven her long before. Very mournful this ending. It is a little victim to consumption whom Meilhac and Halévy show us, terribly miserable, incredibly pretty, upon her knees ; she clasps her child in her arms and smothers him with kisses, then fades away, saying such sweet, pathetic things. . . . And they make us weep over it all, the rascals !

I wept, or at least I had a great inclination to weep ; but I protest against an ending which takes advantage of my soft heart—a little more, and I should accuse them of melodrama ! And yet I am quite wrong ! For what else, I beg of you, could they do with Froufrou ? Let her live on ? No, no, I do not want her to live on— with this incurable wound of a dreadful memory —a penitent in the eyes of her husband, who would never forget and who, being a man of not very sensitive nature, would let her see that he remembered. . . . And, then, a serious, grave, austere Froufrou would be Froufrou no longer. Or if Froufrou remained Froufrou in the depth of her heart, why, in that case, despite the severity of her lesson—you can never tell with little women of her kind—who knows but she might begin again? Beyond a doubt, it is better that she should die. Death, Death in its mercy, saves her for ever from her own frailty and leaves us with memories but of her grace and sufferings. And then Froufrou is just a thrill, a breath of wind, a rustling, a thing of a moment. I cannot imagine an old, not even a mature, Froufrou. I prefer that she should die.

And the moral? There is none. The play is just life as it is, with no shadow of a thesis in it, just truth and some tears and, all-pervading, the fair-mindedness of an indulgent moralist, who sees things as they are. Sartorys is an excellent fellow—there is nothing wrong with him except that he married Froufrou because he loved her and that he loved her too well; this little doll of a Froufrou has in her a fund of loyalty and courage; Louise is perfection itself; Valréas is a gallant man; Brigard is not very estimable as a father, but he has a good heart. . . . And yet, see the outcome of the relationships of all these worthy people : miseries, despairs, and death :—

>   *" Personne n'est méchant et que de mal on*
>   *fait ! "*

That is the moral of *Froufrou*, if you must have one. In short, this play, so modern and so Parisian, is at the same time as widely human as it can be.

[11th October, 1886.   Vol. I.]

V

La Parisienne.   A Comedy.   By M. Henry Becque.

A S we are in the very thick, just now, of the literature of brutality, and as, moreover, the majority of our younger writers are manifestly imitators of M. Becque, why should I not talk a little about *La Parisienne,* recently performed in the house of a lover of letters, by Mme. Réjane (an incomparable Clotilde), M. Antoine, and two amateurs, who played with much ease and naturalness. The piece, of course, is well known, but it is, I think, one of those which gain with age, and it seemed to me that I came to understand better the other day both its originality and its strength.

I would beg you, first of all, not to confuse it with the lugubrious *fumisteries* of the Théâtre-Libre. Not that one cannot find in M. Becque the feeling of which I spoke just now and which has existed perhaps in all ages, but which is particularly characteristic of ours. This feeling —a strange one, at first sight, very intelligible when looked into—consists in the discovery of a delicious intellectual pleasure in the recording of all that is most lamentable in life. La Rochefoucauld, La Bruyère, Chamfort, almost all the moralists and almost all the writers of comedies, have known this pleasure well. But to-day people are revelling in it. It is a malady, a madness—a mode. Almost all the young people who are taking up authorship despise mankind and mankind's existence with a superb light-heartedness. The fatalities of the flesh, the brutalities of our instincts, the grotesque irresponsibility and egotism of all the world—what a sensuous ecstasy is being experienced in noting and depicting all this ! There have been thousands of books about prostitutes and many elaborate monographs upon imbeciles. Why ? Because the writers think that in this way they give proof of their vision ; they think, doubtless, that it is more difficult to descry evil than good and that they display thus an intelligence more free from trammels, more sagacious, more powerful. And, then, disdain is an enjoyment in itself, being one form of pride. And there is yet another thing less obvious, less avowable.

H. BECQUE

One's sensations are titillated by the spectacle of what is ignoble, and especially when the flesh is mixed up with it : this, some theologian will tell us, is merely an outcome of original sin. Or else one feels vaguely (without having any definite intention to profit thereby) that the evil fatalities observed in the world absolve us in advance and place us at ease with ourselves, and then we take a pleasure in seeing only these and in adding to them. There is, moreover, in the kind of nihilistic philosophy to which the recording of these things leads us, the keen joy which belongs to revolt and to negation. (Unless, indeed, we be naturally good and this same nihilism raise virtue still higher in our own eyes and enhance its price while taking from it all outward foundation. . . .)

In short, and contrary to superficial appearances, pessimism is full of sweet consolations. Schopenhauer was not at all bored with life. Our pessimists construct out of their vision of the world works of art with which they are greatly pleased, which sometimes are beautiful, and which bring in to some of them the means of living in comfort. It is only the pessimism of the Christians which is sincerely sad, and which impels to asceticism and renunciation. But, as you may suppose, it is not of this that I want to talk to you.

To return to M. Becque, those who know him declare that his pessimism is of the essentially jovial kind. He is not, indeed, credited with a great measure of kindliness in his judgments upon people and things, but I am told that there is a real impartiality in his malevolence, as it embraces everything—that he is disinterestedly fierce, and out of pure love of art. He enjoys his own cruellest witticisms so much, people assure me, that he laughs before he writes them and while he is writing them and after they have been written, and the artist's joy he gets out of them robs them of their bitterness. . . . He is a misanthrope at the top of his voice, and he scorns the universe while holding his sides.

But it must at once be added that this species of gaiety is carefully disguised in his theatrical work. Nothing can be imagined franker and more simple in their downright vigour, nothing closer to actual truth, than the dialogues of *La Parisienne*. The characters in it are you and I. The things they say are the things we all say daily, naturally, without thinking about it.

H. BECQUE

And these things, which are so natural, are monstrous things. And it is M. Becque's merit to have made us realise so fully that they are both the one thing and the other.

I noted all this, but too cursorily, two years ago when *La Parisienne* was revived at the Renaissance. You will remember those sayings which have so much truth in them and are so terrifying almost, but the meaning of which seems to escape those who utter them—those moral enormities given out in the calmest manner by people who have had the most excellent bringing up and who do not pass for knaves— remarks which open your eyes suddenly to the deepest depths of human folly and hypocrisy, and which make you examine your own conscience and ask yourself whether you might not have said just such things yourself : with the result that you are no longer quite sure whether you are, after all, such a decent fellow ! " Resist, Clotilde, resist ! " exclaims Lafont. " By remaining true to me you will remain worthy of admiration and honour. The day you deceive me——" " Take care ! " cries Clotilde. " Here comes my husband ! " . . . And that other saying of Clotilde's : " You are a free-thinker ! I believe you would get on very well with a mistress who had no religion! How dreadful!" . . .*

You will find utterances of this kind in *Turcaret*, in *Maître Guérin*, in *Monsieur Alphonse*, in *la Petite Marquise* and in *Madame Cardinal*. But it is the originality of *La Parisienne* to be composed almost entirely of them.

I have expressed myself badly. The great originality of *La Parisienne* is that, the theme once taken (it needed some finding), the piece could not be a tissue of witticisms of this kind. As in the case of Molière's Charlotte and Argan, the savour of the dialogue lies in the circumstance that the characters imagine they are expressing sentiments which are quite laudable, or at least legitimate, but which, in reality, are base. The humour lies in the contrast between the estimate which they cherish of themselves and that which we form of them—between what they believe themselves to be and what they are.

Now, *La Parisienne* is so conceived that this contrast is inherent and that the author does not have to seek it. He has only had to place his two principal characters in a situation which is socially immoral, while preserving the senti-

---

* A few lines have been omitted here, as being somewhat unintelligible in English without elaborate annotation.

ments and prejudices which one has in situations
that are correct and regular. The contrast here
is permanent, therefore, and not just accidental
as in other comedies. The author, so to speak,
has only to give the characters a free rein : they
are, from the nature of the case, comic in the
extreme the moment they open their mouths.

Previously, in dramas or comedies dealing with
adultery, the *ménage à deux*, the *ménage* of the
husband and wife, had been taken as the starting-
point. Then came along the lover, or lovers,
and the action opened. And sometimes (and it
was thought to be " the limit ") the piece would
end with a tranquil and enduring *ménage à trois*.
This is the point at which M. Becque's comedy
begins ! He starts off with the *ménage à trois*
(the husband, the wife and the lover) solidly
established and regarded, at least by the lover
and the wife, as a normal and regular institution.
Lafont, the lover, is a second husband, a husband
de cœur, as it were ; du Mesnil being a husband
de raison. Mme. du Mesnil has dreamed of an
existence in which her duties to the world should
be all fulfilled without her heart being sacrificed.
And Lafont, for his part, thinks of himself so
much as a husband that he cannot bear to see
Clotilde frequenting the society of women of easy

virtue ; and when she says to him, in allusion
to one of her friends : " Are you going to blame
Pauline for merely doing for M. Mercier what I
do for you ? " he not only replies, as one might
expect : " That is not the same thing " ; but
when she asks where is the difference, he answers
very seriously, and after some deliberation : " I
see a difference." And we may be sure he does.

The comedy which we are accustomed to see
played between the husband, the wife and the
lover is played here between the lover, the wife
and the second lover ; and—a matter for
rejoicing !—it is played to the advantage of the
husband. For some time past Lafont has noticed
something strange and mysterious in Clotilde's
conduct ; he is jealous and he makes just the
kind of scenes her husband ought to be making,
and at last she sends him packing. The fact is
that Clotilde, a little tired of her two consorts,
the legitimate one and the illegitimate, has
" taken a lover," M. Simpson—her first lover by
her reckoning, her second by ours. But, as she
is, after all, a well-disposed wife, she turns
Simpson to good account and is able to put
du Mesnil " on to a good thing." Then Simpson
vanishes from the scene. Clotilde, who has some
vague remorse over her conduct, not towards

du Mesnil, but towards Lafont, becomes reconciled with the latter. And the regular *ménage*, the *ménage à trois*, resumes its functions in the most correct possible style. There is nothing changed. Or, rather, yes! The position of the husband *de cœur* has been notably ameliorated. Simpson's off-hand ways have made Clotilde appreciate Lafont's devotion and sincere affection; and he promises to be jealous no more—and keeps his word. All, therefore, has been for the best.

Moreover, Clotilde has deceived her husband *de cœur* only to secure a lucrative appointment for her husband *de raison*. Oh, yes, she is a worthy little woman. She feels *that*. Her conscience does not prick her.

You can gauge the enormous comic value which such a situation, such a sense of moral security in what we still call immorality, must give to the conversations of Clotilde and Lafont—without their having to raise their voice and without the author having to underline his points. I do not know any comedy more continuously and naturally ironical than *La Parisienne*. And here is something still more rare. After we have laughed over the contrast between the sentiments of Lafont and Clotilde and their real situation, their tranquillity sets us reflecting; and, were

E

it not for the solid principles with which we are furnished, we would say : " Well, after all, as this little arrangement makes them happy, is it not better that they should believe it to be in accordance with the rules that govern society ? Is not their illusion a beneficial one ? They retain their prejudices, whilst living as though they had none. Is it not at once the highest practical wisdom and the finest tribute (although a roundabout one) to the moral code ? "

Thus, the simplest words uttered by Lafont or Clotilde give us, at the least, two successive and contradictory impressions which end by fusing into a veritable philosophic doubt. When, seeing her husband looking downhearted, Clotilde says to him sweetly : " Come, cheer up and don't look so miserable. What would you be like, supposing a real misfortune happened to you ? Supposing you lost me, for instance ? "—our first feeling is of amazed amusement and we exclaim to ourselves : " Well, certainly she has the cheek of the devil ! What a misfortune it would be for du Mesnil to lose a wife who deceives him with this serenity of mind ! " And then we reflect : " After all, it *would* be a misfortune for him. He has found her company agreeable and she has been a good comrade to him. She has had his interests at heart. She does, indeed, deceive him, but she is so clever that he has no suspicions. And it may even be asked whether she does deceive him. She loves him in her own way. Only, as she happens to have the two husbands, she is obliged to let them go shares. . . ." And this makes one feel that it would be amusing to conceive another piece which should be a pendant to *La Parisienne*. Instead of the legitimate husband being the useful one, as in this case, and the illegitimate husband the pleasing one, the order of things might be reversed and we might imagine a little woman with a frivolous, brilliant, romantic, unpractical husband, a husband to play with, or if you like a husband *de cœur*, and a lover who is sensible, deliberate, serious—much more serious than the husband : a husband *de raison*. . . . But perhaps such cases are not unknown already? Alas ! there is nothing that is not known !

What is certain is that half the people, women as well as men, who are scandalised by Clotilde's lack of self-criticism can be so only through an equal lack of self-criticism on their own part. What is this Clotilde really ? A little animal who has remained, at bottom, as near to nature as the young fauns of mythology, who lived only to be happy and to take their pleasure peacefully wherever they found it.   No doubt, this little animal lives her life in a society hemmed in by laws and usages and conventions ; certain beliefs have been inculcated into her, certain ideas and prejudices.   She speaks the language of these ideas and prejudices, she regulates her outward bearing by them, and perhaps in all good faith. But fundamentally she remains untouched.   She does nothing but satisfy her senses while outwardly respecting a heap of rules to which she submits without understanding them. . . . She is, then, nothing but an eminently expressive example of a class of women whom you have often met. Religious and social institutions are much more material and external things than one imagines. I mean by this that many human beings accept them because they must, from habit or from interest, but without being in the least impregnated by the ideas and beliefs on which these institutions are held to rest.   This kind of little woman will go to Mass, observe all the *convenances*, profess any number of prejudices, air definite and respectable opinions on a host of subjects, and even be really *honnête* or, when not *honnête*, seem to cherish the feelings of those who are ; in short, she will present the appearance in every way of a civilised person, of a Christian, of a moral and reflective human being, and yet she may be absolutely devoid of heart and brain and nothing but a little creature of instinct and emotion. . . . I wish to say no ill of these little women. They can be charming. Look at Clotilde. She is neither foolish nor depraved. She manœuvres with much skill in and out between her two husbands and her lover, and she allows us to see that she enjoys it all. And, on the other hand, she is liable at moments to feelings of tenderness and even of sadness—just as though she had a soul. And she is sensible. She has a circumspection and sang-froid about her which must afford much security to those who come to love her. This type of pretty little human animal is often prudent, middle-class, well educated. Lucrezia, Saint Theresa, Sœur Rosalie, had a loftier conception of life. But which of us would be put out if Clotilde were to cross our path ?

There are millions of such beings amongst us for whom no morality and no religion really counts, although they follow ingenuously certain social rites ; and who must be entirely useless for the attainment of the ends of creation, if creation has really any ends to attain. Clotilde is a curious variety of this genus. In other words M. Becque, in *La Parisienne*, presents to us clearly and with power the most astonishing individual deviation from the morality in vogue that has perhaps ever been seen in the theatre. What higher praise could I give him ?

[18th June, 1888.   Vol. III.]

VI

Ambigu : *Les Gaietés de l'Escadron*. A Play in
nine Scenes. By MM. Georges Courteline et
Norès.

I ENJOYED *Les Gaietés de l'Escadron* greatly.
During the first few scenes, I felt some
prickings of conscience. These lazy *sous-
officiers*, these rascally soldiers, who are so much
given to lying and freebooting, these endless
courts martial and police-court proceedings and
punishments, these coarse gaieties, all this
appalling rowdiness and vulgarity, these low
blackguards who are put before us in the guise of
bons enfants and whose ways and weaknesses are
supposed to call forth our sympathies ! . . . I kept
saying to myself : " Is this really the army ? Is
this, at any rate, barrack life ? And if it is, ought
we to have it told ? And told on the stage of a
popular playhouse ? "

But, little by little, the great surge of M.
Georges Courteline's humour swept over me, and
I came to realise that one must not judge these

things like a moralist in his study. Certain conditions of life modify, no doubt, one's perspective of good and evil. In these agglomerations of robust males shut up in barracks it is inevitable that a certain brutality should evolve. The young soldiers drop back into cheerful savages, into schoolboys of a barbarous school, into children. And the absorbing minutiæ of discipline promote this return to childishness. On the other hand, the discipline being of the most stringent description and utterly opposed to nature, it is intelligible that all the faculties of their minds should tend to fail them and that (without their giving much thought to the matter) everything should seem to them permissible in revolt against a form of rule which they have had no choice but to accept. Hence things that might take on the aspect of criminality in the eyes of a man fully conscious of the fact which binds him to the community, may seem to the ordinary run of soldiers just a good joke or a smart trick. . . . The welfare of the world at large having taken their liberty from them without their consent, they, by way of unthinking protest, take liberties in return. It is nature's revenge against the artificial constraints of military existence. . . . We must be indulgent to them, therefore, and remember that we live under a form of government which does not permit of any certainty that individuals are repaid in full for the things of which they are deprived.

And that is why I was conquered by the time we reached the episode of the Canteen—and even before. This scene diffuses an immense animal well-being which really, at bottom, is quite innocent. First there is the shoving and pushing and elbowing about. Then we have the drinking and singing and shouting and the resounding smacks and thumps and all the familiar interchange of chaff and slang. . . . Oh, yes, it is stupid and noisy and unrefined enough !—one has to get used to it. But one does get used to it ! It is all so redolent of full-blown physical health and strength and one becomes acclimatised and enjoys the atmosphere ! We remember the long, unsophisticated *pomponettes* of the days when we were twenty, when all the pleasure consisted in being alive and in affirming the fact by yells and songs and peals of laughter over nothing and by the unceasing contact of our palates with alcoholic and aromatic beverages and by the putting of extravagant strains upon the functions of our stomachs : a very logical conception, as these functions are life itself and are everything to us. . . . I know, of course, that to be able at a mature age to take pleasure in looking on at these juvenile and loutish delights one must have in one a strain of commonness. But I believe I have.

In any case, even if all this indecorous merriment of the Canteen had left me cold, I should have forgiven the authors everything for having shown me Captain Hurluret and Mme. Bijou.

Captain Hurluret is delicious in his frustrated virtues and his foul-mouthed benevolence. He is Vincent de Paul in a pair of riding-breeches. With horrible oaths and ferocious threats and rollings of the eyes and the fierce outbursts of the timid at heart who believe always that people are making fun of them, he lets the men do everything they want, forgets to punish them, shuts his eyes to their misdemeanours and is at pains to cover them up and make them good. In order to save those gallant troopers, Laguillaumette and Croquebol, from being confined to cells as deserters, he upsets an inkpot over the register of " decisions," and declares that their leave was for four days. Two scallywags, having robbed Mme. Bijou, the *cantinière*, of a stew of bacon, he says to himself that the poor devils, if they are charged with the offence, will get five years' penal servitude and that that is a lot. So he wants to reimburse their victim out of his own poor pay, and Mme. Bijou, who was his *bonne amie* twenty years ago, melts, and the two of them agree to settle matters amicably, and the whole scene is just exquisite. Himself the son of a *cantinière* and a regimental farrier, an *enfant de troupe*, risen with difficulty from the ranks, still a Captain at fifty, perpetually chewing his big moustache, this good old ruffian of a Hurluret, as the Inspector-General, a former messmate, will say of him, has the heart of a *grisette*.

The General's own heart is much less tender. He is the type of the really efficient officer in high command, distinguished-looking, courteous, a trifle blasé and detached in manner, but a man who will stand no nonsense and who on the parade ground will single at a glance the one soldier who hasn't got on his braces. It is a matter for wonder, and for pity, to see how, with his unfailing eye, he detects all the little irregularities which have escaped the notice or been given the connivance of Captain Hurluret, and to hear his sarcastic : " That is of no importance." There is a delightful scene, very accurately observed, in which the Inspector-General casts such a spell over the men that they acclaim first

as " not bad," then " quite good," and finally
" tip-top," the soup which one of them, more
venturesome and self-assertive than the rest, had
begun by condemning as " muck." But as this
Inspector-General (doubtless, in the contentment
of mind due to his consciousness of superiority)
does justice, if a trifle disdainfully, to the naïve
goodness of his old comrade Hurluret, and as,
for all his success, he condescends to absolve that
reprehensible old laggard, we do not mind so
much his brilliancy and superiority. And I
applaud, just here, the sagacity and equity of
MM. Courteline and Norès. Discipline is necessary, but there are times when its application
may be unjust and inhuman. It is well, therefore, that the Hurlurets should temper their
inhumanity, but it is well also that Inspector-
Generals should control and correct the humanity
of Captains " with the hearts of *grisettes*." We
need both the Hurlurets and the anti-Hurlurets :
it is well that the rules which govern the community should be violated ingenuously by God's
children when these rules are in any way unjust
or harsh, and that they should be maintained by
our statesmen in so far as they safeguard us.
And so all is for the best !

[Vol. IX.]

VII

PALAIS-ROYAL : *Les Maris d'une Divorcée*. A
Comedy in three Acts. By MM. Hippolyte
Raymond and Jules de Gastyne.

THE first act of *Les Maris d'une Divorcée*
pleased me by its simple-minded fun.
We are at Chartres. Mme. Claire, a
decent little sort of woman belonging to the
bonne bourgeoisie of the town, was given a slap
across the face by her first husband, the architect
Durosier, who, however, is a very decent sort
himself. She divorced him and has, this very
morning, taken a second husband, M. Paul
Brémond, in his place.

The theme of the comedy is concerned, first
with the obsession of both the wife and Husband
No. 2 by memories of Husband No. 1, and,
secondly, with the wife's return to No. 1, of whom
she was really quite fond and against whom she
had, in fact, no very serious grievance, as the slap
had been no sooner given than repented. . . . She

had petitioned for her divorce in the first flush of her indignation.

The architect Durosier is a good-humoured *bon vivant*, a round tub of a man with a little côterie of congenial and convivial friends of his own type, among them Pommereau, a retired horse-dealer, and Chamouillet and his wife, who have given up business as hosiers, and their son Oscar, a wag with many social gifts—he imitates all kinds of musical instruments and sings comic songs, some of them composed by Durosier himself, who in his own way is a wag also. There is the famous ditty entitled " Duck and Green Peas," for instance. . . . " I never roared so much in my life ! " Pommereau, when he heard it, would declare.

Pommereau and the Chamouillets are put out over the divorce and second marriage of their friend, Mme. Claire. All their habits and customs have been upset. Their minds go back regretfully to those delightful dinners at Durosier's—what a wine cellar he had ! What merry evenings those were, all the company sitting at their ease ; what good stories they all told ; and how their sides shook as they listened to young Oscar and his musical imitations, and as they all joined in the chorus of " Duck and Green Peas " !

RAYMOND AND GASTYNE

They have been round to Mme. Claire's new domicile to see how the land lies there ; they have questioned her old servant as to the characteristics of this M. Brémond. A dry sort of stick they fear he is. Well, they will soon see. M. and Mme. Brémont have not been many days installed *chez eux* before Pommereau and the Chamouillets invite themselves to dinner—" to pot-luck, as in the Durosier days."

Brémond who is, in truth, the dry stick they feared he would be, greets them frigidly, but what does that matter to them ? They make themselves quite at home. Once they are seated at table the talk is all of old times and of " *ce brave Durosier*." They persist in referring to Claire as Mme. Durosier and soon are inadvertently addressing Brémond by his predecessor's name. Brémond himself, flustered and bewildered, ends by calling his wife Mme. Durosier.

Young Chamouillet's turn comes with the dessert. He has donned a pierrot costume, having to take part later in a performance in the house of some other friends. He is in his very best form. Taking up one of the chairs, he draws forth from it the deep notes of a violoncello. He is great ! The ex-horse-dealer bangs the table in his delight. M. Chamouillet makes a gobbling kind of noise—it is his way of laughing. And Mme. Chamouillet loosens her bodice. . . .

I must admit that I found all this very refreshing. One of my several selves—for we have several selves, all of us—most decidedly belongs to this set and has a real relish for this form of merriment. In its ingenuous way the piece is just a sample of the lower strata of Gallic gaiety : a bit of *blague*, very elementary and very gross, any amount of impudicity (the rock-bottom of our *esprit national*) and, above all, an immense delight in living. This kind of inane exuberance is scarcely conceivable except round a table and after dinner amid the exaltation induced by wine and in an atmosphere of tobacco smoke. I feel that it would not be impossible or unpleasant for me to take part in it. Oh, those tremendous jokes, those shaking sides, those mouths gaping wide to the ear and deep down to the heart ! There is (never mind the contradiction in my words) a real exhilaration in all this mass of mirth, a sense of relaxation from the effort of thinking— I mean for those of us who think we think. . . .

And, after all, they are not too bad, these jolly lunatics. There is a drunken kind of magnanimity, one feels, in Pommereau. The Chamouillet couple have committed no crime—not even stolen except in accordance with the etiquette of commerce; they cherish all the correct prejudices, without knowing why. They are very severe on Madame So-and-So, " who has got herself so much talked about ! "· If their son turned out wrong, they would don sackcloth and ashes and, as they are avaricious, they would die of it, but they would go to confession first. There are worse types in the world.

We all have Chamouillets among our relatives and acquaintances, and (especially after dinner, when for an hour or two they are at their best) we must open our heart to the ordinary run of people, with their banality and triviality, for the simple reason that they constitute almost the whole of mankind.

[4th April, 1892. Vol. VII.]

VIII

LA RENAISSANCE : *Spiritisme*, in 3 Acts. By
M. Victorien Sardou.

THIS month has brought us three
important plays, all of which have
been remarkable for their various
merits and all of which, while pleasing us in
the first place, each on its own account, have
had the effect of delighting us, taken together,
by their very variety, and as an illustration of
the astonishing diversity of minds perceptible in
this period of commendable literary anarchy.

In *Spiritisme* we have a brilliant manifestation
(for the sixtieth time or thereabouts, don't
forget) of that famous *adresse* of M. Victorien
Sardou which has won him so much glory, but
which has also done him injury at times by
obscuring his other qualities. In this instance
his achievement consists in extracting a drama
out of a matter which our cheap scepticism and
trivial mocking minds tended to make us regard

as a theme rather for vaudevilles. And that is not all. He has contrived to write a play more than half of which is made up of long discussions of spiritualism, but the action of which does not go to prove that spiritualism is either true or false and in which the spiritualistic beliefs of one of the characters serves only as a dramatic means of bringing about, suddenly, the *dénouement*.

Mme. Simone d'Aubenas, a woman of thirty, whose nature is by no means bad, and who does not detest her husband, a good fellow, is yet in an unsettled, dissatisfied, bored kind of mood ; she is suffering as they say *du vague à l'âme* (but her soul's trouble is not really vague, it is clearly marked enough), and she has fallen in love with a handsome Walachian, Michael de Stoudza, who has crossed her path. The evening we are introduced to her she ought to take the train home to her *château* near Poitou, where her husband is to rejoin her in the course of a few days. She goes to the station with one of her friends, Thecla, who is in her confidence, lets Thecla travel off alone and makes her way, through side streets, to the little house in which the Walachian is expecting her.

Now, the train which she ought to have taken collides with a goods train laden with petrol.

SARDOU

The passengers are all burnt to death. Simone's jewellery-bag has been found on Thecla's body, and M. d'Aubenas has come to believe that the corpse is that of his wife. Mad with grief he takes back with him the charred remains.

Simone learns these particulars next day while still with her Walachian. How the tidings are imparted to her, with what feelings of surprise and terror and despair she hears them, I leave it to you to imagine. After writhing with grief and dismay, she asks herself what is to be done. To show herself to her husband is to confess all. Very well, then; as she must pass for dead she may as well turn her predicament to good account —she will go off with her Michael into his poetical Walachia, where they will live happily. But this is not at all to the mind of Michael, for Simone d'Aubenas is no more; this is a penniless Simone whom he now has to do with, and the one he wanted was a Simone divorced and wealthy. The fellow reveals naïvely enough his ignominy of mind, and Simone gives full vent to her contempt and disgust for him.

So there is nothing for it but to confess everything to her husband. . . . But now we have M. Sardou up to one of his tricks; or rather we have a fine example of the manner in which he is always ready to sacrifice probability to the requirements of his plot—that is to say to the exciting of our sensibilities : we should be ungrateful if we condemned him for it ! Just at this very moment we hear behind the scenes a melancholy chanting of the Prayer for the Dead, and Simone, through the half opened window, sees, walking behind the coffin in which he believes her dead body to be contained, her husband, his body bent with grief, his feet giving beneath him, great tears coursing down his cheeks ! We feel that the sight will overcome her—that by an irresistible impulse she will fling herself down at his feet. We are almost tempted to cry out to her : " That's right ! Show yourself ! You will be able to think later of things to say, and, even if you don't, no matter ! " The poor man's misery, as he walks there behind the hearse, with the appalling memory of his wife's burnt body imprinted upon his mental vision, is worse than can be the discovery of a sin which she will have begun to expiate in the very act of avowing it. " Besides," we want to say to her, " you are in no condition to weigh things in the balance. Have pity therefore on this unhappy husband of yours ; show yourself—if you are a thing of flesh and blood and not a mere puppet worked by wires to evoke our anxiety and keep us in suspense ! " But Simone does not show herself. She will confess, she is resolved, but not now ; later, when it will suit her : and, in order to spare her husband, she will leave him for another week or fortnight—I don't know quite how long—a prey to profound despair and to that dreadful vision of death ! For M. Sardou has a *dénouement* up his sleeve—the only *dénouement* he will hear of. And as it is all for our delectation we acquiesce !

This *dénouement* turns out to be very ingenious. You must know that M. d'Aubenas is a believer in spiritualism. Coached by a cousin of hers who has made himself her adviser in the matter, and attired for the part, Simone " appears " to her husband one night, the moon shining on her face, in a great empty hall, and he takes her for a ghost. She confesses her unfaithfulness to him and, without any great pangs, he is able to forgive the wife whom he imagines dead. We are very indulgent to the dead whom we love. We reproach ourselves for not having loved them enough while they were with us. Their sweetness and goodness seem to us now inestimable because we shall never know them more. On the other hand, the sufferings they caused us have faded away like themselves—they, too, have vanished. We forget the harm they wrought us, knowing there can be no more of it. And then the " never again " revives our happy recollection of the departed ones while the unhappy recollections are effaced.* And then we pity the dead merely in that they are dead, just simply because we love life and we feel that their lot might have been our own. Perhaps it is really a kind of deep pity for ourselves that drowns so easily our rancour and resentments !

It is, then, quite natural that d'Aubenas should pardon his dead wife. Simone proceeds : " But would you give her your pardon were she living ? " And, bit by bit, as he notes the moving tones of this voice, and the sobs and passionate gestures of the phantom, d'Aubenas realises that Simone lives ! Her offence takes life with her and becomes real and poignant—it no longer has the slightness which it owed to the seeming impossibility of its recurrence. And, then, it cannot be easy for this votary of the occult to condone tranquilly the stratagem of

* One feels that Jules Lemaître may have been thinking of the young wife whom he married in 1881, when he was a Professor in Algiers. She died early. It had been a luckless union, but he thought of her with tenderness after her death.—F. W.

this false apparition—the anger of the betrayed
husband might well be intensified by the indignation of the " believer " who has been duped. . . .
Certainly, but we have the notion that this good
fellow would in such a case have looked a trifle
comic and, as spectators, we should be distressed
and disappointed ; so we are relieved when, in
the sequence of feelings which now ensues, the
unhappy man burns his boats and a sudden
impulse of forgiveness leads to his embracing the
living woman within the arms he had opened to
her shade.

But to what purpose, then, are the discussions
regarding spiritualism which fill nearly the whole
of the first act and half the third ? Obviously
these stage conversations cannot solve the
question for us. They leave me still in doubt.
I say to myself, " There is something in it " ;
yes, but what ? I do not know whether investi-
gations into spiritualism have ever been made
under scientific conditions. I remember only
that those high priests of spiritualism whom I
have met have seemed to me credulous and little
able to defend their tenets. And, assuming that
one does accept as true the discoveries of these
people, it astonishes and depresses me to find
that the departed spirits evoked are even more

mediocre than living beings and that spiritualism brings us back—or very nearly so—to the naïve conceptions of Homer, to those Cimmerian regions wherein the pale and languishing spirits of the dead do but continue their terrestrial lives in a manner diminished, benumbed, meaningless, and that they have nothing to teach us survivors except dissatisfaction with the idea of thus surviving. And, on the other hand, it does not in any way matter to the action of the piece whether spiritualism be true or false : it suffices that M. d'Aubenas believes in it. All these discussions, therefore, are meant merely to amuse us. As, however, they do amuse us, all is well.

Only, all might be still better. The last scene but one in the third act is really fine. This consists of a talk between M. d'Aubenas and Simone's cousin in which M. Sardou, with moving eloquence, expounds the very ancient doctrine of the purification of souls in successive existences, and, linking with his doctrine the theory of spiritualism, holds out before us a law of goodness and forgiveness and mutual assistance between the living and the dead ; so that the universe of souls—some attached to terrestrial bodies, others floating around us or already departed for other planets, in proportion to the stage which they have reached in their long expiatory pilgrimage—resembles a vast " Communion of Saints." And the apparition of Simone, although false (and all too like the comic apparitions in *Erreurs du Mariage*, when one comes to think about it), pleased me, all the same, by its mysterious grace. Quite seriously, if these last two acts of *Spiritisme* had been written in Norwegian and had then come back to us, translated from Norwegian into German and from German into French, it is not impossible that they would have seemed to our young critics quite peculiarly Norwegian and have called forth their most intolerant enthusiasms.

And, thus thinking, I begin to regret that M. Sardou, instead of using spiritualism merely as a stage-device to bring about a climax, did not really make it the theme of his play, and that in his plot he did not introduce communications, imagined to be real, between the dead and the living. It was not necessary for this, that we ourselves should be spiritualists : it would have sufficed that the author should seem to be one and that his faith should interest us. We would gladly have lent ourselves to this device. We would only have asked M. Sardou, in return for our goodwill, to tell us a story at once human and mysterious and with a strangeness in it that should alternately set us trembling, weeping, and dreaming. What kind of story? We should have left that to him.

[Vol. X.]

IX

THE VAUDEVILLE : *Le Prince d'Aurec*, a Comedy
in Three Acts.   By Henri Lavedan.

THE evening was delightful—a trifle intoxi-
cating even.   There was a sense of battle
in the air.   To the pleasure of applauding a work so elegant, so brilliant, so vigorous, as
Le Prince d'Aurec, was added that of applauding
for the defence.   For, as you know, the piece
had its opponents before ever it was played.

An old gentleman who, one knows not how or
why, has been elevated by the wiseacres of the
Press and the clubs to the rank of *Arbiter Ele-
gantiarum* (not in the field of morals) had,
apparently, declared that " Society would place
the Vaudeville in quarantine." And someone
connected with a journal which aspires to the
glory—not, in truth, very great—of being the
organ of the *gens du monde*, had added that the
play would be hissed off the stage before it reached
the end of the first act.

These notions are too ridiculous for it to be

credible that they were really entertained. But in any case—and hence the sensation of conflict which mingled so stimulatingly with our enjoyment—one was conscious of a feeling of antagonism on the part of a certain number of spectators, an anxiety to avail themselves of any opportunity that might present itself for protesting out loud against the piece.

No such opportunity offered. That, perhaps, was because M. Henri Lavedan, while exercising to the utmost his rights as a dramatic author and as a free agent, did not go a single yard beyond them. There was an expectation that he would give us portraits and indulge in personalities : he did not. And yet in *Le Prince d'Aurec* we had the keenest and, towards its conclusion, the bitterest and most thoroughgoing satire at the expense of the weaknesses and queernesses and vices, the absurd futility and folly and corruption of our *noblesse*, or what remains of it (I speak, like M. Lavedan, in general terms, and I know there are exceptions, both in the country and in Paris) ; and it had, in addition, the further merit of being the first satire, at least upon the stage, to show us the baseness of the last representatives of the race of *gentilshommes* measuring their wits against another baseness, that of our

94

LAVEDAN

Money-Kings, and the two types coming together in a fashion which is in itself a baseness, considering the circumstance in which it is done. Here we had a theme which was truly of to-day and a theme worth handling ; and to say that M. Lavedan has shown himself equal to it is no slight praise. For this is to say that he has put into it not only all the wit of which he is capable —and that is much—but that he has put into it also other things besides wit.

Yes, it was a fine theme. Reflect that the continuance—inevitable, of course—of an aristocracy by birth in the midst of a democracy is one of the strangest and absurdest of social phenomena. All the *raisons d'être* of an aristocracy of this kind having been gone for more than a hundred years, its rôle in life having completely ceased to exist, its privileges having been abolished, our noblemen continue none the less to live their lives incongruously as noblemen. *La vie noble* having been taken away from them in all its essence, they persist in the old attitudes which belonged to it, like those specimens of the brute creation which are subjected to experiments in the physiological laboratories and which after their heads have been severed, continue at least to walk. It may be said that for the last hundred years our aristocracy, *quâ* aristocracy, has had a reflex existence. Necessarily these attitudes which it has preserved are simply and solely the set attitudes of the *ancienne noblesse*, their outward forms, with all the ceremonies, all the escutcheons and liveries appertaining thereto, all their social exclusiveness, their grand air, their airs and graces. Not desirous and not capable of doing anything, unfitted for even such work as they would not think beneath them—in art or letters, for instance—and scornful of all work which would in any degree derogate from their high station, powerless in politics, they have directed their intellectual faculties towards the only uses for which they suffice : social functions, racing, fencing, driving four-in-hands, designing new styles of ties and waistcoats—finally, roulette and baccarat. . . .

Now, they could not keep up this kind of life for long ; and as, for more than a century, they have been spending without earning, the malady known as impecuniosity would end by freeing us of them. . . . It is here, however, that comes into play the conjunction of the two kinds of baseness above mentioned.

And in this conjunction it is the vanity of the *bourgeois* and of the plebeian that is the most to be blamed. For you see (and this is unavoidable) the whole of our rich democracy, and even a portion of our democracy which lacks riches, remains incurably dazzled by that which it continues, in spite of everything, to regard as the *noblesse*. Dead and buried as a political class, the *noblesse* still lives—indeed, as a social caste, it flourishes, I fear, more than ever. And the superstition which it inspires in the hearts of *parvenus* is all the stronger, perhaps, because it does not rest on any effective power but only on memories, absolutely empty conventions, sheer nothingness. Imaginary values, the values based merely on opinion, are the most secure of all as they stand in no danger from contradiction by reality. Yes, the nobility is all the more alive in a sense, for having outlasted the organisation which was its *raison d'être* by reason of the opinion which it has retained of itself and by the way it has succeeded—herein lies our shame—in making so many of us share that opinion.

We run after those things which we appreciate. Now, observe : never has the mania for titles of nobility raged more lamentably in the French *bourgeoisie*, and with it that mental malady which declares itself by the usurping of the particle " de," although this particle has heraldically no significance. Oh, no, Poirier has never ceased to dream of being a Baron. The prestige of a title impressed tradesmen and merchants to the point of nullifying their business sense. And our functionaries—our *gens de place*, as we used to call them—are no better in this respect than the tradesmen. It is not merely on the stage that a Radical deputy regards a Marquise as a superior being.

And so things fit in marvellously. Just at the moment when debts and imminent pennilessness make the survivors of our nobility turn their eyes towards the Money Kings, the vanity of the Money Kings inclines them in favour of the survivors of our nobility.

This vanity is a very stupid and very odious thing, for it implies the most fallacious view of life, and the most extravagant admiration for what is least deserving of it—for that which is worthless save in the eyes of public folly. But it is a vanity reinforced by the universal sanction of imbeciles. And so we have a financier who has become a multimillionaire. He has risen from very low down. He has begun perhaps by being the business adviser of a smart woman of the town—I am here improvising the biography of the banker in M. Lavedan's play, as M. Lavedan has not given it to us himself. Then, perhaps, he married the ex-manageress of some Family Hotel who had saved a tidy sum. This he knew how to turn to good account. Then we lose sight of him for ten or twenty years. He is away in Syria or Persia or somewhere. He returns with an enormous fortune, which henceforth increases almost automatically until by means of big deals it has grown to ten times the size. Our man is now a great personage. He has estates everywhere, an historic *château*, a gallery of pictures, as many mistresses as he wants. There is only one thing lacking to him—to be " in Society." His supreme ambition is to be in Society—real Society : in its innermost, narrowest, most distinguished circles, those most redolent of the Faubourg St. Germain. Penetration into this sphere is now in his eyes the one and only thing desirable, just because it is the one and only thing which presents some difficulty to him. He has everything else except this : this, therefore, he must have—it is essential to him. In order to attain this his insolence will descend to any servility and his avarice will throw money out of the window. . . .

In M. Lavedan's comedy, the *noblesse* is called Prince d'Aurec and the Money Kings are represented by Baron de Horn.

THEATRICAL IMPRESSIONS

Prince Dominique d'Aurec is a young man of thirty-five whose characteristics and mode of life —precisely similar to those of some hundreds of our *gentilshommes*—are as follows : Elegant but played out, keeping as fit as he can by means of fencing and visits to the spas. Educated at a Jesuit college. Relatively moderate in his financial affairs, between his eighteenth year and his marriage he bled his mother to the tune of 1,100,000 francs only. Since his marriage he has swallowed up two aunts and a grandmother and his wife's *dot*. How has he spent all this money ? On nothing, apparently—just on gambling and dressing well and, in short, in being the Prince d'Aurec. He has one individual trait : he is not a dupe of the conventions and traditions which he represents. He knows that the nobility's rôle in public life is finished and done with ; he laughs at the history of France and at all her Kings and Queens and Princes ; he has a Constable's Sword among the family relics at home : it is his family's most venerated possession— their " *Croix de ma mère*," he says laughingly. He fully realises what a poor creature he is, and how futile. But he makes out a defence for himself with a species of bitter humour. For— a second individual trait, this—he has *esprit*.

In fact, he has all M. Lavedan's *esprit*, which seems very improbable, but which does not detract from our enjoyment !

Then there is his wife, the Princess, a splendidly dressed-up doll, crazy about dress, amusements—and notoriety ; but not without virtue altogether, as we discover eventually. She is always putting on her clothes, but at least she does not take them off. After allowing us, throughout most of the play, to believe she is no better than a wanton, she reveals her better self in the *dénouement* and, perhaps through atavism, displays a pride and a courage without stain.

Then there is the Vicomte de Montrejault, known to his intimates as Jaujault, a nobleman from Brittany, son of a Chouan, who spends all his time organising *pavanes* and who is addicted to sentences without any verbs : a supremely comic transformation of the Marquis so familiar in Molière.

We have, too, the old Marquis de Chambersac, who, having lost all his money, has become an *agent d'affaires*—an *agent d'affaires* for people in Society, of course. He gives advice to inexperienced *parvenus*, takes a hand in the sale of old pictures, brings about meetings, sometimes innocently, sometimes not. But remaining a *gentilhomme* all the time, without the loss of the least atom of his dignity and distinction.

There is one good woman among all these corrupt personages, one honest and ingenuous and energetic human being among all these backboneless creatures : the Duchesse de Talais, mother of the Prince d'Aurec. The Duchesse was born Virginie Piédoux, daughter of a very successful butter merchant. While quite small, she became a votary of the *noblesse*, and, thanks to her father's ten millions of francs, she married into it. She has preserved her social creed ; she believes in Louis XIV, she believes in the Constable d'Aurec, she believes in the essential superiority of blue blood. The kind of talk her son indulges in horrifies her. Her personality presents a blending of native commonness, a dignity acquired by dint of goodwill and of conviction of her high standing, and a credulous but inoffensive pride coupled with a sort of humility, for, despite everything, she remains persuaded that the one incomparable honour that has been bestowed on her, in a life often secretly sorrowful, was that of being married to the wretched fellow rejoicing in the name of Duc de Talais. She takes refuge in the cult of the great ancestors of the family. And thus, through an irony which is almost touching, the only person who, amid all her vanities and absurd illusions, has yet preserved a true conception of what the *noblesse* used to be and ought to be—the only person who, all things considered, represents worthily here the aristocracy of birth, is a butter-merchant's daughter.

The representative of Money is a Jew, Baron de Horn. I do not need to tell you that I have no kind of prejudice against the Jews. The Israelites are an extraordinary race whose history is the most beautiful and most tragic in the world. And in their origin they were an extremely noble race, a pastoral and warlike race. . . . Like that exile in the story whose misfortunes had made him a " Pole," the modern Israelites might say : " It is our misfortunes that have made us Jews ' " " Jews " in the popular and un complimentary meaning of the expression. For centuries Christian Europe forced them to excel in the business of money-making : they are not to be blamed for this. Therefore I have no animosity against them. We owe them our Divinity, and their women are often marvels of charm and wit : I am grateful to them for these things. Moreover, there are still some of them who are not millionaires. They are a race which is prolific, indeed, of stockbrokers but also of musicians, and vaudevillists, players, poets—decadents, too, and neuropaths ! Some of them come to love France as much as we do ; and then they rank as Frenchmen like ourselves, exactly like ourselves—and all the more that our French blood, you must remember, is an incredible mixture of bloods of every description. If we were to be strict on the subject of racial origins only the Beaucerons, of whom I am one, could strictly be called French !

I feel certain that M. Lavedan is of the same mind as I am on this subject, and that if he has circumcised his Money-King he has been moved to do so only by his sense of the dramatic requirements, for a banker on the stage is not completely a banker if he is not a Jew. This is reason enough for me, and I seek no other. Moreover, if M. Lavedan has attributed to the Baron de Horn a vanity and ambition which are unbounded, if he has given him the soul of a bandit and something of the hatefulness of a Shylock, he has made him neither a fool nor vile. My only complaint is that he allows Baron de Horn to admit here and there the superiority of the aristocrats by birth—this humility on his part seems to me improbable. I feel that a Jew—and the same remark applies indeed to a Christian—who has made 100,000,000 francs will always reckon himself the equal of a Prince d'Aurec. No doubt he will realise that he has succeeded in getting the Prince to receive him only by overcoming a very strong prejudice ; this prejudice, however, will seem to him but one of the most foolish of all prejudices. Before the tribunal of his own inner consciousness, he will never admit that it has anything to justify it.

Apart from that, the insolent Baron de Horn strikes me as a very plausible creation. He believes in nothing but the power of money : therein we have his whole personality. It follows that if he himself is base he believes firmly in the baseness of everybody else. And, in point of fact, he is justified in this belief of circumstances. It is this power that has opened to him the doors of the d'Aurec home and many other such doors in succession. He calculates even that this power will open—let me say the heart of the Princess. And the Princess has given him grounds for so calculating. When she accepts from him a cheque for 250,000 francs to pay her dressmaker and her draper, is it for the Baron to suppose that she sees only in this transaction the deed of a friend—or, rather, a delicate way on his part of evincing his gratitude for the honour done him in receiving him ? Is it credible that she can be so stupid as not to realise that such services as these impose an obligation on a woman ?

Just as he has a hold on the wife, Baron de Horn has a hold also on the husband. Already over head and ears in debt, Dominique d'Aurec has lost 400,000 francs quite recently to the Prince de Souabe. On this coming to the ears of the Duchesse de Talais, there is a scene between her and her son—a scene which would lose some of its humorous effect perhaps if it were enacted elsewhere than at a fancy-dress ball (*he* attired as the Constable d'Aurec, *she* as Mme. de Maintenon), but which would gain in dramatic intensity. For it is admirably conceived, this scene : the Duchesse all trembling with an exasperation not entirely free from vulgarity ; the Prince incensing her by his frigid raillery, making fun of his ancestors, making fun of his family name, ending with a threat to sell the " Constable's Sword "—the old Marquis de Chambersac has offered him 130,000 francs for it !

But this sum being insufficient, the Prince has recourse to his good friend, Baron de Horn, in the *entr'acte* which ensues.

The first two Acts of the piece are Comedy

pure and simple. They are sparkling with *verve*, a *verve* at once imaginative and incredibly picturesque. One scarcely notices that there is a certain slight lack of action in them. In the last Act we have Drama—a settlement of accounts.

The Duchess has stuck to her guns; she has refused to pay her son's debts. She has carried him off, and his wife also, to her estates, and they are dying of boredom there. She, for her part, is disenchanted with the Nobility! And she explains her feelings to an old friend in words that are singularly moving. But we must pass on. If I were to pick up all the pearls in *Le Prince d'Aurec* I should never be finished.

Baron de Horn follows the d'Aurec couple into their provincial retreat, and, as the Princess persists in her air of being unable to understand what he has in view, he tells her straight out and quite brutally. Now, at last, all her aristocratic feeling comes to the fore and she repels him in tones of the loftiest pride. He reminds her that she is in his debt. Three hundred thousand francs, a mere trifle! . . . The Prince appears at this moment, and the two men confront each other. The Prince has enough princely sentiment in him to wish to turn the insolent money-grubber out of the house, but Baron de Horn sits down in an arm-chair. " Your wife owes me three hundred thousand francs ; you owe me four hundred thousand. That makes seven hundred thousand. At that price I confess I calculated I could get into the Jockey Club and have your wife. No Jockey Club for me, however, and no Princess. I am swindled. You call me a Jew. It is you who are the Jews." And he proceeds to develop this proposition quietly with the help of numerous and precise arguments. The Prince is beside himself with rage. At last the worthy Duchesse, who has been told by her daughter-in-law what has happened, reappears on the scene to tell the Baron that she will pay. " You know," he remarks as he leaves, " I've got the Constable's Sword as well ! " The Jew has the last word. This climax ought to please the children of Israel. It should please other people also. . . .

The Baron gone, Prince d'Aurec professes himself transformed by the ordeal. He declares he hopes there may be a war, so that he may show at least that he knows how to die. " Like the rest of us," observes a friend of the house, Moncade, a novelist. " *Il y a manière*," replies the Prince.

It is Moncade who is right, I think. I do not

LAVEDAN

believe that even in war there is any special manner, peculiar to the *noblesse*, in which death is to be sought and braved. But the phrase is a success, and it illustrates M. Lavedan's moderation and his anxiety to hold the balance even. Yes, whatever may be said on the subject, the author of *Le Prince d'Aurec* has been studiously just. Open an old book, *les Caractères* of la Bruyère, at the chapters dealing with " Gifts of Fortune " or with " the Court " or with " the Great," and you will see that of the two writers, la Bruyère and M. Henri Lavedan, it is not the latter who is most severe either on the men of money or the *gentilshommes*. Note, too, that the Princess—in spite of those unwise borrowings which suggest either that she is an imbecile or a " bad lot "—proves herself in the end a woman of virtue ; that the Prince is contemptible without being a dishonest man—this distinction, which may seem absurd, agrees exactly with the facts ; and that the Jew's only crime (at least in the play) is to hope to corrupt a woman who has exhibited all the symptoms of corruption. It is, indeed, thanks to this moderation in the portrayal of individuals that the satire in the piece takes so wide a range and that, partisanship being conspicuously absent, its bitterness becomes so formidable. *Le Prince d'Aurec* is one of the most remarkable social comedies which we have yet seen. No one could have succeeded better in making us see and realise how, because the *Noblesse* is for sale in the open market, Money annihilates it and does well to annihilate it. And now, who will annihilate Money ?

[6th June, 1892, Vol. VII.]

X

PORTE-SAINT-MARTIN : *Les Bienfaiteurs*, a Comedy in four Acts. By M. Brieux.

IN the Pleiad of our young play-wrights, M. Brieux occupies a place singularly honourable and apart. The others are all Parisians and *blasés* and as guileful as the Devil. M. Brieux is no Parisian, either in mind— he has no gift for *blague*, that is to say for irony practised for its own sake ; or in his choice of subjects. *Blanchette*, *Réboval*, *l'Engrenage* are provincial comedies, while his first effort, *Ménages d'artistes*, was notable, I remember, for a kind of wholesome good nature which seemed almost extravagant on the stage of the Theâtre Libre. M. Brieux, unlike most of our more brilliant writers, distinguishes between good and evil very surely and very clearly, and he likes to impress upon us the fact that he makes this distinction. He has something about him of a Bonhomme Richard and of a Simon of Nantua, for he does not seek out subtle and unusual cases, he is not afraid of the commonplaces of ethics, and how wise he is in this ! All his pieces are didactic comedies—I am almost tempted to call them " moralities." " We should not give girls of humble parentage the kind of education which unfits them for their station in life." (*Blanchette*) ; " Pharisaïsm, even when of good faith, is not virtue." (*Monsieur de Réboval*) ; " Politics are a great source of corruption " (*l'Engrenage*). Every one of his pieces is, from beginning to end, and without straying from its path, a methodical demonstration of each of these truths. M. Brieux, in this way, would be apt to recall a little too much that irritating Boursault or that melancholy Destouches were it not that by his simplicity and spontaneity and his dramatic talent, he sets us thinking much more still of our excellent Sedaine, whom he resembles moreover in his lack of style. But his chief originality appears in this : his mind is not audacious (that is all too easy) but brave ; he brings it to bear on the study of great questions, the questions which interest the entire human community, and he does so with the air of a self-taught man looking at things with fresh eyes and possessed of a very warm heart and a very clear faculty of judgment. But at the same time, this candid preacher is a most accurate, most minute, and sometimes most penetrating observer of average humanity. Thus he contrives, I don't know how, to infuse colour and flame into the most frigid type of dramatic productions. His " moralities " live. That is what is most extraordinary about them.

In *Les Bienfaiteurs*, then, we have another didactic comedy, lit up luckily by its author's power of satire and of observation and by his ardour for what is good. It begins, and develops, like a *conte moral*. A " money king," dropped down from the skies, places his millions at the disposal of the engineer Landrécy and his wife, Pauline, and enables them to try to realise their dreams of " charity "—a " charity " which they make the mistake of confounding with the various forms of alms-giving. I don't know how anyone can say that the idea of the piece is confused and vague. The whole play goes to show the inefficacy of " charity " when administered in a spirit of worldly-wise patronage, and the undesirable results which it is apt to entail both for those who bestow it and for those on whom it is bestowed. It is a series of scenes, each one of which proves a point in the thesis.

H

THEATRICAL IMPRESSIONS

One section of the play depicts for us in succession, 1° the vanity, 2° the pretentiousness, 3° the lack of discernment, 4° the folly, 5° the hypocrisy, 6° the jealousies, etc., etc., of the ladies who go hustling and bustling over " good works " ; another, the haughtiness, the hardness and the coldness of the cautious, distrustful type of " benefactors," and so on and so forth : we are shown how " benefactors," male and female alike, are demoralised by the methods in which their " charity " is practised. Other scenes illustrate the way in which the people succoured are demoralised simultaneously through these same methods ; we are shown how their bitterness and their envy are intensified, and how this kind of charity, preoccupied with picturesque " cases "—" repentant prostitutes," " converted convicts," etc.—provides chiefly for the idle and the vicious, the liars and drunkards, and overlooks the honest and industrious poor. The result of it all is that a poor mother kills herself and her three children, while Pauline's charitable ministrations bring relief to women who trick and swindle, and that, in spite of increased wages and new schools and clinics and orphanages and benefit societies, Landrécy's employees, whose demands have increased more and more in proportion to the concessions already made to them, go out on strike. . . . And the Money King smiles cynically at the two-fold failure of his friends.

The carrying-out of the idea struck me as very unequal. There are a number of scenes which might have been written, it seemed to me, by another hand. While some scenes go rushing like a torrent, full of life and palpitating with reality, others are artificial, " made to order "; they are like scenes laboriously con- trived to illustrate a sermon.

The living scenes include the one in which the baggage, named Clara, brings it home to the honest poor woman Catherine—who gets no help as she is at work—what an advantage it may be to be unmarried and on the streets when you have a child to provide for; and the one in which Féchain, the lost sheep that has been found, confesses that he has never really been in jail and that he has borrowed the criminal record of a pal in order to qualify for the favours reserved for ex-convicts; and the one in which the leaders of the strike first discuss matters with Landrécy, and then deliberate among themselves, landing themselves in their stupid rebellion, out of bravado, out of mutual distrust and fear, out of the intoxication induced in them by certain high-sounding revolutionary words—unmindful of the sacrifices of their employer, not so much because they have always viewed them as interested sacrifices as because they have never been made conscious that he is a man with a heart. . . . Yes, all this part of the play is excellent—with honest and effective wit in it and a truth to life which takes strong hold of you ; but I could find no trace of this truth or of this tone in the two interminable meetings of the charitable dames. Even the scene in which some of these absurd persons welcome the workers into the drawing-room and, affecting airs of familiar friendship, offer them Madeira and cakes, seemed to me all wrong, not in the conception but assuredly in the setting and the execution. Here, and in other places, the author quite manifestly has forgotten to look at life. . . .

Such as it is—with its superior qualities and with its defects, which at least are frank—the piece, an extremely interesting one, would not be without harshness (for, after all, these mala-droit benefactors are well-intentioned, almost all of them ; and to give badly is better than not to give at all, and one might suppose that,

as Augier says, the only quite new thing M.
Brieux has to tell us about charity is that we
must not practise it) were it not that the real
thoughts of the generous-minded author are
made as clear as the day in two scenes which
are made to serve as pendants to each other.
The first is that in which the workman Plu-
vinage comes to Landrécy, seeking sympathy
and advice, and is quickly got rid of with a
five-franc piece. And the second is that in
which this same workman, his wife dead, returns
in his distress to his employer and the latter,
honestly moved, holds out his hand to the poor
man and takes him sobbing in his arms. These
two episodes are not perhaps the most " outstanding " in the play, but it will not be denied
that the lesson which they inculcate is irre-
proachably definite and distinct.

It is the lesson that charity, or, more properly
speaking, alms-giving—even were it abundant,
which it never is, and even if it were not organised
with more red-tape than the functions of a
Government Department—can serve no purpose
by itself and that kindness must go with it :
kindness and open-heartedness and a friendly
relationship between the rich and the poor.
One scene (which unfortunately was omitted)

shows how much of pride and of instinct for domineering there is, without her being conscious of it, in Pauline's charitable craze : Pauline wants to make a young cousin of hers marry the " money king " in order to save the " good works " from failure through lack of funds, letting us see thereby how devoid she is of simple goodness. . . .

But perhaps humility also would be welcome. In a story which I have read and which followed out an idea similar to that of M. Brieux, a man of wealth who had been addicted to lavish and contemptuous charity, having at last come to realise his mistake, expressed himself thus : " One must serve the poor poorly, as Pascal said. One must enter into the hearts of the poor, not despise them for sinking to a level of mind to which we ourselves also might have sunk if we had been oppressed by the same necessities. One must at least love them for their resignation, these folk who so out-number us and who could, if united in anger, sweep the rich off the earth like bits of straw. One must not, while helping them, be revolted by their misery, but accept it as one accepts the mysterious designs of Him Who alone knows the reason of things. For the aim of the universe is not the production of plastic beauty, but of kindness."

This, it is true, savours a little of Christian mysticism. Like everyone else, I accept as good the more laical conclusion of M. Brieux. And I may tell him that a beginning has been made towards putting his idea into practice. In London—and now in Paris, also, I am assured—some fair dames have sought to live on terms of friendly intimacy and equality with the women and girls of the poor districts. They have a building, a kind of modest club, in which they meet and talk with them and give them tea and cakes, and to which they go in their smart dresses to show that there is nothing forced or constrained about their actions and that they come really as friends. Each of these ladies singles out one of the poor women with whom to gossip and exchange confidences and whom she addresses by her Christian name. And I am sure that some excellent souls bring to this task a touchingly good faith ; but, for the few who find in these meetings the real joy of " simplifying " their own life, what a flock of foolish females there must be, one fears, who seek in them merely an opportunity to s'encanailler, and who go to them in the same sensation-seeking spirit in which they might go to Bruant's or the Moulin Rouge! And one wonders in what spirit the loose little persons of Popincourt resort to these meetings and what kind of remarks they make about them afterwards!

Ah, yes! How hard it is, first of all, to practise charity to the extent one should, and secondly to practise it in the way one should, and with efficacy! Or, rather, it is a simple matter enough and the Gospels tell us what to do. Only it is annoying that, quite apart from the egotism infused into every man with his life, the economic conditions of our vast modern societies and the wall they build up everywhere between the rich and the poor, render it impossible to put the Gospel teaching bodily into practice. In order that there should be no more wretchedness, it would be necessary that all men should be very good—they should *all* be good, and *extremely* good. Now this " extremely " would involve the throwing aside of almost everything, it would involve consecrating our lives to others, it would almost involve our becoming saints. Thus mankind would approach the extinction of wretchedness in the same measure as it grew perfect morally, and its spiritual and economic salvation would prove to be one and the same thing—the same ideal to be aimed at, the same goal to be reached.

It is well to think about that ; and the work of M. Brieux, which forces us to think about it, at times with anguish, is worthy of esteem and of praise. Go and see this comedy by a painter, who is often excellent, and by a very good man ; you will be by turns amused and, in the finest sense of the word, edified ; and into the bargain you will have at certain moments the delight of applauding against something or against somebody.

[Vol. X.]

XI

PORTE-SAINT-MARTIN : *Cyrano de Bergerac*, a
Drama in five Acts, in verse, by M. Edmond
Rostand.

I WAS not present at the first performance
of the *Timocrate* of Thomas Corneille,
nor even at the first performance of
Casimir Delavigne's *Vêpres Siciliennes* when
the audience kept up its applause uninter-
ruptedly throughout an entire *entr'acte*. But
this at least is true : *Cyrano de Bergerac* has
made by far the biggest "hit" that I have
witnessed during the thirteen years (all but a
little) that I have been plying my trade of
dramatic commentator.

The whole Press of the day after and the
whole Press of the ensuing week proclaimed
Cyrano a *chef-d'œuvre*. And here is something
even more worthy of note : M. Rostand's piece
has turned into a veritable Pindar one of our
most eminent and most intellectual critics.
It has sent M. Emile Faguet into a fit of

prophetic frenzy. He has assured us that *Cyrano* is " the most beautiful dramatic poem which has appeared for half a century " ; that a great poet has emerged " who at twenty-five inaugurates the Twentieth Century (already ?) in a brilliant and triumphant manner . . . the herald for us of a new era upon which the eyes of Europe will be fixed with envy and those of France with an ecstasy of pride and hope ! " Almost trembling with emotion, our austere and masterly reconstructor of all the philosophical and political systems of the last hundred years proceeds to exclaim : " Can it be true ? The end has not been reached ! There shall be again in France a great poetical literature worthy of 1550, worthy of 1630, worthy of 1660, worthy of 1830 ! It is here—it is at hand ! I shall have lived long enough to see it ! In my yearning to see it in its fullness, I shall begin to dread death ! Ah, how delicious, alike the hope and the fear ! " . . . Thus spake Joad of the New Jerusalem !

Alas ! All my eulogies, however warm and however heartfelt, will languish beside these, and will look to the author like roundabout disparagements. But let us resign ourselves to the task of talking with common sense !

ROSTAND

I shall display the ungrateful courage of considering *Cyrano* as an event, no doubt marvellous, but not, properly speaking, supernatural. M. Rostand's play is not only charming, it has been clever enough to come to us at just the right time. I attribute its prodigious vogue to two causes, of which one (the principal one) is the play's own excellence, while the other is, without doubt, the degree in which the public has been wearied and surfeited with so many studies of psychology, so many trifling tales of Parisian adultery, so many productions by Feminists, Socialists and Scandinavians : all of them pieces to which, *a priori*, I make no objection and among which there may be some that contain as much moral and intellectual substance as this radiant *Cyrano* ; but assuredly less delectable, and in any case their numbers overwhelmed us a little. The fact that an eloquent journalist could exclaim that *Cyrano de Bergerac* "*éclatait comme une fanfare de pantalons rouges*," and that it had set on foot a revival of nationalism in France, proves clearly enough that ideas and instincts somewhat alien to Art have had their share in the triumph of this romantic comedy and that when a success of these dimensions is achieved everything helps to swell it out !

I hasten to add that the timeliness of its production would have been of but moderate service to M. Rostand's piece if it had not been in itself of a rare and surprising merit. But what really is the nature of this merit ? Is it really true that this comedy " inaugurates " a century, or, more modestly, that " it makes a beginning "—like *le Cid*, like *Andromache*, like *l'Ecole des Femmes*, like *la Surprise de l'Amour*, like *le Mariage de Figaro*, like *Hernani*, like *la Dame aux Camélias* ?

I should be tempted rather to believe that its merit is that, instead of inaugurating anything at all (or so it seems to me), it prolongs, combines and blends in itself, without effort and most assuredly with *éclat* and even with originality, three centuries of comic fancy and moral grace—and with a grace and fancy which are our own.

For in the first Act, all this gay tumult of actors and poets, of *précieux*, and of *burlesques*, of *bourgeois*, and drunkards and purse-snatchers, of all the Court gallants and literary Bohemians of the day of Louis XIII—what is it really but a dream of the good Gautier, which has been

realised with a skill beyond belief and upon which
the author of *Capitaine Fracasse*, gazing at it
from up above (where he is bound to be), must
bestow a brotherly admiration and benediction.
Has not Cyrano, together with something of
Matamore in *l'Illusion* and of Don Japhet
d'Armenie, the aspect of a Rodriguez and a Don
Sancho ? Scarron could not have emitted at a
single breath or with that abundance of imagery
Cyrano's wonderful disquisition regarding his
own nose ; and the ballad of the duel sets
one thinking of Saint Amand revised by
Théodore de Banville with the help of Jean
Richepin.

In the second Act we are in the lure of Maître
Ragueneau, which might be that of the Radis-
Couronné and in which the Cadets de Gascogne
carry themselves like so many Sigognacs. Cyrano
appears ; and as he has the most beautiful mind
in the world with the most luckless countenance
(" *Noble lame—Vil fourreau* ") one is reminded of
Hugo's antithesis, of Quasimodo and of Triboulet
and also of Ruy Blas—" *ver de terre amoureux d'une
étoile.*"

Here begins the very graceful drama—a drama
of the psychology of heroism : one of which
Rotrou and Tristan and the two Corneilles would

have been glad to have had the idea, which most
certainly is up to the level of their most " gallant "
and delicate inventions, and which would have
rejoiced the idealistic sensibilities of the Hôtel de
Rambouillet with its nobility and pride and
tenderness. Roxane, a *précieuse*, the object of
her cousin Cyrano's unspoken love, has given him
a rendezvous. What she has to say to him, alas !
is that she loves a handsome fellow, Christian de
Neuvilette, who has just joined the Company of
the Cadets de Gascogne and for whom she
implores Cyrano's protection as the Cadets are
inclined to make a butt of him. On hearing this
avowal and entreaty, which pierce his heart,
Cyrano flinches no more than would a hero of
l'Astrée. Chaffed by Christian regarding his
nose, he has the strength to restrain himself and,
when the cadets leave them alone, he opens out
his arms to his fortunate rival. Christian is good-
looking but he has little wit—he does not know
how to talk to a *précieuse*. No matter ! Cyrano
will provide him with conversation, " soft
nothings," and will write his love-letters for
him. . . . Don't say that this reminds you of a
situation in *la Métromanie*, for if the poet Damis
provides Dorante with the verses which the latter
sends to Lucile, the mistress of his affections,

ROSTAND

Damis does not love Lucile and therefore it is not the same thing. M. Rostand's invention is Cyrano's sublime and yet voluptuous self-sacrifice in consenting to help his rival to victory : Cyrano consoles himself with the thought that, after all, it is his own heart and his own wit which will be loved, without her knowing it, by him whom she adores. Here, assuredly, we have the utmost extreme of selflessness in love. . . .

And with what grace this sentimental comedy is contrived ! It is evening, beneath Roxane's balcony. Christian, left momentarily to his own resources, can say only : " I love you ! " and our *précieuse* thinks it inadequate. But Cyrano, in the shade, prompts Christian, and Roxane begins to think that her lover is progressing. Then, for convenience' sake, Cyrano, disguising his voice, himself addresses her ; and his declaration, begun in the stilted phraseology of convention, ends in the style and rhythm of Victor Hugo :

" Oh ! mais vraiment, ce soir, c'est trop beau,
    c'est trop doux.
  Je vous dis tout cela ; vous m'écoutez, moi, vous !
  C'est trop : dans mon espoir, même le moins
    modeste,
  Je n'ai jamais espéré tant ! Il ne me reste
  Qu' à mourir maintenant ! C'est à cause des mots
  Que je dis qu'elle tremble entre les bleus rameaux !
  Car vous tremblez comme une feuille entre les
    feuilles ;

I

Car tu trembles ; car j'ai senti, que tu le veuilles
Ou non, le tremblement adoré de ta main
Descendre tout le long des branches du jasmin."

Roxane is moved by all this melodious
fervour ; her heart opens out ; and Cyrano,
to his rival's profit, has transformed the
précieuse into a woman. She invites Christian
to come up, and, while the two lovers stand
upon the balcony in each other's arms, their
heroic Galeotto, down below, murmurs dolefully
and yet not without some secret sweetness in
his heart :

" Baiser, festin d'amour dont je suis le Lazare
Il me vient dans cette ombre une miette de toi ;
Et, oui, je sens un peu mon cœur qui te reçoit,
Puisque, sur cette lèvre où Roxane se leurre.
Elle baise les mots que j'ai dits tout à l'heure."

And then the fantasy takes a fresh departure.
A ruse borrowed from the pleasant tradition of
our oldest repertory allows Christian, thanks to
the credulity of a good Capucine, to wed Roxane
almost in the beard of Guiches, who also loves
her. Guiches, to avenge himself, sends Christian,
with Cyrano still as his comrade, to a post of
danger in the war ; and we are now introduced
to the camp of the Cadets de Gascogne and, as
they are poor, we see them fighting in rags and

tatters though, spiritually, they are fighting in fine lace.*

Cyrano, meanwhile, having continued to write to her in Christian's name, Roxane, a *précieuse* no longer but with a heart now set on fire by his epistles, sallies forth in a carriage to rejoin her husband and at the same time to bring the famished Gascons food. And the episode might almost be taken from the Fronde and worked up by Dumas *père* in that lively and resourceful way of his.

And now Christian takes his revenge and suddenly shows himself the equal of his friend in sublimity of sentiment. Roxane has said to him that, by reason of his letters to her, what she loves in him now is not the beauty of his face but the beauty of his mind and heart, and she has thought to give him pleasure by her words. But his mind and heart are the mind and heart of Cyrano. "It is no longer I whom she loves," says Christian to himself; and, unable to bear this false position in which he has been placed, not liking to keep a love which he feels he has stolen and yet not bearing to risk its loss, he goes into battle resolved, quite simply, to meet his

* M. Lemaître borrows here a phrase from Georges d'Esparbès, " *la guerre en dentelles.*"

death—in the thought, doubtless, that thereby he will be Cyrano's equal, at least in his heart. And as he does not wish, even when dead, to benefit by a lie, he is constrained to reveal to Roxane everything : but his lips grow cold ere he can speak the words and from what you know of Cyrano you may feel assured that he will respect alike Roxane's illusion and Christian's secret.

But, in spite of himself, Cyrano reveals the secret fifteen years later in the garden of the convent whither he repairs nightly to visit the grief-stricken Roxane. One night the sweet-faced young widow gives him to read the last letter which she received from Christian ; and Cyrano, who knows it by heart, " reads " it easily although darkness is falling ; and it is thus she identifies him as its real author and discovers his magnanimous and exquisite self-denial.

> " Pourquoi vous être tû pendant quatorze années,
> Puisque, sur cette lettre, où, lui, n'ètait pour rien,
> Ces pleurs étaient de vous ? "

And Cyrano, handing the letter back, replies :

> " . . . Ce sang était le sien."

And, having met with a mortal injury from an accident an hour before, he dies, resting his back

against a tree, the moon shining full on his face—
that dear moon, planet of dreamers and vision-
aries, in whose realms he was wont to wander!
He dies cleaving with his idle sword, and with
Alexandrines which might perhaps be spared, the
spectres of Lying, Cowardice, Compromise, Prejudice, Stupidity, like any good Romantic from
Richepin or Victor Hugo ;—a luckless lover, one
who loved by proxy and went unloved ; an
imperfect poet, to be pilfered from presently by
the unblushing Molière ; but happy to have so
nobly dreamed, to have made protest by the
sheer splendour of his soul against the calamity
of his face and of his fortunes and to have
kept his plume—his *panache*—flying, even in
death. . . .

This adventure of Cyrano and of Christian,
with the conception which it implies of love, with
its prides, its ingenious scruples, its capacity for
graceful self-abnegation—I can think really of
nothing to equal it in our drama down to the time
of Racine. Neither in subtlety, nor in delicacy,
nor in sentimental heroism are Cyrano and
Christian surpassed by Alidor in *la Place Royale*,
or by Pertharite, or Pulchérie, or Attale in
Nicomède, or by Eurydice or Suréna, or by
Timocrate. It is almost as though the literature

of preciosity were now giving us at last, after two hundred and fifty years, its true comedy. I can think of nothing to compare with it except the *Carmosine* of Alfred de Musset.

Thus, to summarise all I have been saying, if one passes in review the succession of forms of art and sentiment which M. Rostand has harmoniously called back to mind, we shall see that they extend from Honoré d'Urfé's romance and Corneille's first comedies down to the *Capitaine Fracasse* and the *Blorise* of Banville, taking in the Hôtel de Rambouillet, Scarron and the *burlesques*—taking in Regnard, too, a little, as regards his style; and also, if we note certain touches of romantic grace, the *Prince Travesti* of Marivaux; ending with *La Métromanie*, the fourth Act of *Ruy Blas*, with *Tragaldabas* even, and the novels of Dumas *père*. So that *Cyrano de Bergerac*, instead of being a new departure, amounts rather to a recapitulation, or if you prefer it, a culminating efflorescence, of a form of art which dates back three centuries.

And this—is there need to stress the point?— without any trace whatever of direct imitation. To the innumerable forms and inventions which he recalled without seeking to recall them, M. Rostand has added something : he has added the resourcefulness of his mind and the sensitiveness of his heart, and all that three centuries of literature and life have bequeathed to us in thought and feeling. For, even if we lack genius, we may well succeed in realising, better than they could themselves, the dreams dreamt by our fathers and in distilling their essence. The " picturesqueness " of the time of Louis XIII glows far more vividly for us than it did for contemporaries ; and it was for us to create a " braggart " who should be as pure and tender as a maid and to extract from the " preciosity " of those days all that it contained of the exquisite and the generous. Everything in *Cyrano* is retrospective ; everything, even the modern romanticism which adapts itself so easily to the imaginations of the romanticism of 1630 ; nothing in it, I repeat, belongs to the author except the great and understanding love with which he has loved these visions of the past ; except the voluptuous melancholy wherewith, here and there, in his last three Acts, he colours the things of yore ; except, finally, the things which have made him so capable a playwright and so rare a poet.

And that, doubtless, is the reason—while many people, not all of them blockheads, have been proof against the *Cid* and *Andromache* and

THEATRICAL IMPRESSIONS

l'Ecole des Femmes and *Hernani*, all of which had " something new " in them and the substance of any of which may well have been more considerable, after all, than the substance of *Cyrano de Bergerac*—that, doubtless, is the reason why no discordant voice has disturbed the universal chorus of applause which has greeted M. Rostand's play. This too fortunate effort lacks, then, at least one of the signs by which the empirical critic recognises the work that inaugurates : it has failed to be misunderstood—a matter regarding which, I imagine, the author will easily console himself. If the entire public has given *Cyrano* so fervid a welcome, it is because they have felt its grace, but also because they " recognise " it and because they found in it, brought to a surprising degree of perfection, a form of invention and of poetry which has been, if one may so express it, contemporary for three centuries past and with which they were already in some slight measure familiar. Everything in *Cyrano* charms us and nothing offends us : but there is nothing in it to respond to the most serious part of our intellectual and moral preoccupations ; and if it be true that this very brilliant comedy " inaugurates the twentieth century," then the twentieth century would seem to be already on a down grade.

ROSTAND

What I have said is not aimed at any depreciation of this seductive jewel. There are plays which mark an epoch and which yet are not very beautiful. On the other hand there are masterpieces which mark no epoch. And, in regard to those plays which seem to mark one, it always turns out that that what looked so novel in them, whether in matter or manner, has been at least sketched out in some former work of mediocre merit. This signifies that even without genius one may devise something new and that, even in art and in literature, " novelties " are apt to be in the air, so to speak—in the back of the minds of intelligent contemporaries before they take shape in a masterpiece. What belongs, therefore, to the author of an illustrious work—whether this work begins or continues a series—is but the beauty of which he conveys the impression. But this beauty itself, which we have not created, does it not belong to us in so far as we comprehend it ? Does it not belong to us wholly if we comprehend it wholly ? And at such moments are not we the equals of the poet himself—except on one point, a point of some importance—the faculty of artistic creation which is but a happy accident and which does presuppose some superiority of the mind ? The beauty of a work, being naught if not recognised and felt, is in a sense the work of all the world. A consoling, fraternal theory, and one which has the great advantage of suppressing envy.

M. Edmond Rostand's verses sparkle with joy. Their suppleness is incomparable. Sometimes— and I make no complaint of this—it is pure virtuosity, the art of putting into verse no matter what, witty *tours-de-force* and poetical fireworks : but, more often, it is a beautiful frenzy of forms and colours, a poetry full of the sunshine—a poetry of the South—so much of the South that its author might hail almost from Persia or Hindustan. Some fastidious persons have been at pains to point out carelessness and weaknesses in his lines. I have not noticed so many as they make out ; besides, they escape attention when one is witnessing the play, and all is atoned for, moreover, by the quick action and the grace. M. Rostand overflows with metaphors and ingenious comparisons, full of a pleasant affectation and of a delectable " bad taste " ; he talks as naturally as possible alike the language of the *précieux* and that of the *burlesques*, which at bottom are the same ; and what offended me in *la Samaritaine* ravishes me here by its close kinship with its subject.

ROSTAND

In the rich rôle of this arrogant, gorgeous, mad, magnanimous, jovial, tender, subtle, ironic, heroic, melancholy, and I know not what else, Cyrano, M. Coquelin was admirable from start to finish and with an assurance, a breadth, a variety of diction ! . . . In the realm of the expansive and the flamboyant, he is beyond comparison the great classical comedian.

[Vol. X.]

XII

Porte-Saint-Martin : *Messire du Guesclin*, a
Drama in three Acts and five Scenes, in verse.
By M. Paul Déroulède.

M. PAUL DÉROULÈDE is a man, evidently, of excellent feeling. This
excellence has even made him some-
thing of a poet. In the years which followed the
defeat he wrote *Les Chants du Soldat*, several of
which were marvellous little songs of war and
patriotism, with an infectious lilt as of a regi-
ment on the march, and written in a form which
was supple and vigorous, not without lapses into
clumsiness, but which have been condemned
mistakenly for lack of art : any striving after
Parnassian perfection in them would have been
misplaced. That was M. Déroulède's golden
hour. He was then in complete communion with
the great mass of Frenchmen. Since that time
the bond has broken, but it is France that has
changed, not M. Déroulède. France, which

seemed at first to take its duty very gravely, slid away little by little into distractions, into naturalism and pornography and the Universal Exhibition and the barren and abominable pastime of politics, financial brigandage, etc., etc. The poet of the *Chants du Soldats*, for his part, remained true to his dream. And that is why, in this world of the listless and the resigned, of the cynical and the rapacious, he seems to-day unique. The bold gestures which he continues to make astonish. He has all the appearance (I say it quite without irony) of a hero out of work. He presents the aspect of a great monster of a windmill whirling its long arms about with nothing to grind—gallantly, generously, but in vain.

And it is not for him that I feel pity.

He has, moreover, nothing in common with those patriots who, in the neat phrase of Huysman, call out for a revenge, " the remote contingency of which reassures them." He has shown incontestable bravery on more than one public occasion. And they tell me he is charming, and that all his friends adore him. I myself regard him as worthy of esteem and respect.

You are reflecting, I am sure : " Here we have the rhetorician ! Now for a chastisement ! "

DÉROULÈDE

Not at all ! But I have been at pains to make it clear (although it might well have been understood) that, having to sit in judgment on. *Messire du Guesclin*, my verdict on the piece, whatever it should prove to be, would not in any way indicate my feelings as regards the person of the author. I am, besides, convinced that M. Déroulède likes better being praised for his virtues than for his literary efforts. And now my mind is at ease.

If *Messire du Guesclin* had been signed by an unknown name (it is true that in this case it would not have been played at the Porte-Saint-Martin, or, perhaps, anywhere else) I should certainly have passed upon it the verdict which follows—and why should I now pass any other ?

The prologue shows us the Dauphin Charles escaping at night from the Paris of Étienne Marcel in a ferry-boat. . . . A short prologue and somewhat significant.

In the next scene, Bertrand du Guesclin, in his château at Pontorson, receives the Treasurer of the kingdom, Jacques Bureau, who has been sent by the Regent Charles to beseech the help of the Breton leader ; after deliberating with his lieutenants, Bertrand, who is all for the unity of France, consents. The scene has a certain

grandeur. And then " *Aux armes !* " Here we
have a lyrical passage of some beauty, which I
would cite if I had the text before me. Someone
having declared : " We know no fear," a soldier
cries out : " Fear, fear, I defy fear ! " ; now, we
have a moaning and groaning of women who
avow their terror, and du Guesclin himself,
entering, exclaims : " I, too, know fear. He who
knows it not, is no hero ; but I overcame it with
the help of God. . . ." The whole constitutes
a kind of heroic ballad round this theme of
Fear—a ballad which, changing presently into a
prayer, ends up with a demonstration of enthusiasm. And this, without any doubt, is the best
thing, and the most original thing, in the piece.

In the third scene we see another deliberation
in progress—in a hall in the dungeon of Vincennes.
Bertrand du Guesclin holds forth copiously in the
presence of the Regent Charles and of his great
vassals, and prevails upon them to attempt the
retaking of Paris before marching against the
English. At this moment a man, Jean Maillard,
comes to tell du Guesclin how, although a
fanatical believer hitherto in Etienne Marcel, he
has been moved to abjure the Tribune and
assassinate him, Marcel having allied himself
with the English and the Duke of Burgundy.

DÉROULÈDE

The retaking of Paris, therefore, will now be easy. This scene, then, consists of a deliberation and a narrative. The narrative in itself is not without interest. The case of Maillard, a rebel of a simple-minded type, but a true patriot, stands out clearly ; and we do not fail to sympathise with the roundabout condemnation of the Commune of 1871. But, oh, how long this narrative is ! And when are we coming to the drama ?

In the following act . . . well, it is the same thing, more or less. This time it is a deliberation and a parade at arms. It takes place on the eve of the Battle of Cocherel—it might be equally well the eve of any other battle.

Du Guesclin, made Constable of France by King Charles (King John having died in England), imposed his authority upon the recalcitrant *seigneurs* and expounds to them his plan of campaign. He denounces them, at the same time, for their pride, their selfishness, their hardness with the poor, and tells them that " there is anarchy down below because there is anarchy up above " ; and, while asserting that there is need of " a man who shall rule," he gives them at the same time a little lecture upon evangelical Socialism. (This part seemed to me good and

K

145

effectively written.) And then, for the third time, " To arms ! "

The final scene shows us (in that trumpery little cathedral which we saw before in *Jeanne d'Arc*) the coronation of Charles V, swiftly got through. And then : " *Vive la France !* " The epilogue is as insignificant as the prologue. The only *raison d'être* of both is that they are pendants to each other.

But I have forgotten to tell you about the adventure of Julienne, du Guesclin's sister. Julienne is loved by Olivier de Mauny, a spotless knight, the Constable's favourite disciple. But she loves the Gascon soldier of fortune, Raoul de Caours. This Raoul has the gift of speech and he is a man of ideas ; he sympathises with Étienne Marcel. " Perhaps Marcel stands for the future ! " he says. Towards the end he offers his services to the enemy, because his troops are short of provisions and he is kept waiting for his pay. Du Guesclin discovers his treachery and drives him forth, a moment after Julienne has plighted her troth to him. Then Mauny kills the brilliant mercenary in a duel—Julienne, I believe, withdraws to a convent. This adventure leaves us unutterably cold.

To sum up, the drama lacks form and cohesion.

DÉROULÈDE

This succession of deliberations and of departures for the war, of dissertations upon this or that episode in the history of France, of patriotic harangues, etc., might be continued indefinitely. And then, while gladly accepting the legendary view of Bertrand du Guesclin, I should have liked to see some other indications of his character than a touch of roughness here and there. M. Déroulède's du Guesclin might almost as well have been called Bayard or Hoche or even Joan of Arc. As to the verses, they are certainly not as bad as people are saying ; but perhaps they are not always as good nor as beautiful in their " studied simplicity " as the author himself declares in so many " interviews."

I may add at once that the success of the piece on its first performance was sensational. You cannot imagine what shouts and cheers and rounds of applause followed upon the unlooked-for tirades of Messire du Guesclin—I say " unlooked for " only from the standpoint of chronology. It is like this. When on a public occasion you throw certain words to the crowd it would hold itself dishonoured if it did not look profoundly moved. There are poetic lines which demand an ovation.

I have a real relish personally for patriotic

verse, but I enjoy it in proportion to its beauty, and I prefer to read it all alone, modestly, rather than to hear it vociferated from the stage. Therefore I was somewhat uncomfortable the other evening. But on reflection I recognised that this was the hidebound standpoint of a humanist. After all, and apart from all literary considerations, what the crowd was acclaiming was Courage and Purity and Fidelity and Heroism and France and the Army of France ; and these are things, in truth, more interesting and moving than the plastic beauty of verse, even than the depth and truth of dramatic works of art. I came to realise, with a certain emotion of shame, in respect to this audience (in which certainly there were no inveterate voluptuaries and no professional prostitutes, no lying politicians and no ignoble money-grubbers) how much more admirable their feelings were than mine. And then I began to applaud like the rest !

[Vol. IV.]

XIII

Henry Meilhac and His Plays

HENRY MEILHAC is dead. We shall see him no more in the two or three restaurants which he had frequented for forty years past ; nor at the Cirque, nor at the Folies-Bergère, whither he would come to dream at his ease. To dream of what ? Of the frail iridescent little world which he carried about with him in that rounded head of his, so suggestive of a silent, gently-mocking Buddha. For this Parisian who could not do without Paris or, rather, without a certain corner of Paris (a few hundred yards of its pavements, to be precise) had in reality a life, not so austere, but just as retired, just as meditative, just as firmly closed against all that was not his work, just as resolutely set apart, as that of an ascetic, as of some epigraphist of old, or as of a monk of the Institut Pasteur.

That is the reason—and because he had, in

his way, a touch of genius in him—why his theatrical productions will continue, I think, to be regarded as among the most original of his time. In them will be found, more accurately and agreeably than in any others, the manners and ways, the idiosyncrasies and catchwords and turns of speech of the frivolous and elegant society of the Second Empire and of the earlier years of the Third Republic. Now, it is not a matter of indifference to us to know in what ways reputed pleasure-lovers found their pleasure, and what the woman of fashion and luxury was like at different stages of her existence and at different periods of the history of civilisation. It is this species of interest which commends to our notice still to-day the comedies both of Dancourt and of Marivaux.

The plays of Meilhac were unpretentious plays, without theses, without claim to rank as social satires, but with an immediate effect of novelty. They bore no sort of resemblance to the plays of Scribe, whose methods Sardou continued, nor to those of Augier or of Dumas *fils* ; but they were equally unlike the plays of Labiche. Labiche retained much of the burlesque tendencies notable in Duvert and Lausanne, he excluded women almost altogether and really (whatever people

may assert) never got away from farce. Meilhac,
starting out modestly from vaudeville, invented
—apparently with a single stroke—a form of
comedy with less strain and effort in it than
mark those of Dumas and Augier, less artificial
in composition, less " literary " in style, a more
intimate and familiar form of comedy, and even
with more truth in it, despite its occasional
indulgences in buffoonery. So natural a kind of
dialogue, piquant and ingenuous alternately,
had, I think, never been heard before.

Fundamentally, Meilhac was a realist. If we
except two or three imbroglios (such as *Tricoche
et Cacolet*) the action of his plays is always very
straightforward in its unity. He sometimes con-
tents himself with plots of a time-worn, classic
order (*l'Ingénue, Brevet Supérieur*) or with some
quite old-fashioned *conte bleu* (*la Cigale*). His
way of sacrificing as little as possible to convention is to point out convention's trammels
while laughing at them a little. He never passes
convention off for truth. In *Monsieur l'Abbé*,
two characters mistake for a moment each other's
identity ; whereupon one of the two exclaims :
" I tell you what, we are at cross-purposes, but
there is a way of getting out of cross-purposes :
each of us has merely to say who he is ; it is

very simple ! " Meilhac does not mind his plays being condemned as " ill-made " or as including " slices of life " (*le Réveillon*, Act II). In regard to the material " setting " in which he places his characters, his realism is ingenious and extremely picturesque : I shall instance only the concierge's box in *la Boule* at the Variétés, the theatre lobby in *le Roi Candaule*, and the somnambulist's *salon* in *Ma Camarade*. He indulges in *mots de nature* whenever and wherever he feels disposed. He is so sincere that he almost always finds it impossible to bring about his *dénouements* : like Molière. He may even be said to possess a gift of hard and fierce observation—he shows it less often than he is accused of doing, but he was capable of the third act of *Gotte* and the last act of *le Mari et la Débutante*. He founded the anti-Scribist school of play-writing. In many respects he was the precursor of the Theâtre-Libre in the things in which the Theâtre-Libre has occasionally excelled.

But having about him nothing of the pedant, he escaped moroseness by dint of his fantasy. . . . It has become a commonplace to say that the hall-mark of Meilhac is an indefinable mingling of fantasy and truth. The meaning of which is that this very acute observer has a great deal of imagination—and of the imagination of a poet. The librettos of his famous operettes, *la Belle Hélène*, *la Grande Duchesse*, *Barbe-Bleue*, *la Périchole*, are delicious even in themselves and without the music. They are exquisite tales in which a poetical sensuousness mingles with the delicate irony and unbridled fooling. They set one thinking of the philosophical tales of Voltaire, the *opéras-comiques* of Favart and the plays of Musset ; and yet they could be by nobody but Meilhac. They are among the gems of our literature of the stage.

One feels one knows the characters in his comedies. They are extraordinarily alive, and with a life which seems contemporary and quite close to us. The women excel. Perhaps no one has expressed so well as Meilhac the changeableness of women, the caprices, the nerves, the irresponsibility, the grace, the *je ne sais quoi* of women. He gives us little courtesans, sometimes " connected with the stage," and all the little world which buries itself around them (mothers, aunts, manicures, waiters from the *cafés* and clubs). They are all very attractive, whether knowing or *naïves*, smart or silly—futile, untruthful, voracious little persons, but not too wicked. Some of them, the little actress in *Ma*

Cousine, for instance, have only too much heart and are perfectly charming. Side by side with them, or in their midst, we have women of the world and " respectable " women," full of excitements and anxieties and curiosities, but incapable of *grandes passions*, with plenty of wit and gaiety, but little self-knowledge, saved generally from " going wrong " by their sense of the ridiculous and their fondness for " blague " : Mme. de Kergazon in *la Petite Marquise*, for instance ; and Henriette in *Décoré*. Standing out above them all is Froufrou, the adorable, the only one of them who goes all lengths—and she dies of doing so. There are some quite young girls, too, almost all of them very individual in their aspect and in their conduct : Margot and Pépa and " la Cigale," and, in a class apart, Cécile Leguerrouic in *Brevet Supérieur*, a " good " girl, but of Paris—very " representative," indeed, and so true !

And then the men : the sceptical ones and the soft ones ; the colourless *boulevardiers* ; the simple-minded ones and the hot-headed ones, in great numbers ; and the old *marcheurs*, lecherous and credulous : the one in *la Boule* and the one in *Ma Camarade*—I forget all their names and I am writing all this without referring to any books, depending entirely on memories of the past. And this on purpose, so that my impressions may have the more likelihood of being true.

The external verisimilitude of these characters is preserved with a delicate psychology which, for all its air of nonchalance, is sometimes profound. J. J. Weiss spoke with good reason of the " Racinian psychology " of *Ma Camarade.* Marivaux is always being mentioned in connection with Meilhac, and rightly. *Pépa* is simply picturesque Marivaux—Marivaux picturesque and condensed. . . . Nor must we forget that admirable third act of *Froufrou,* wherein every effort of the poor little heroine not to fall is turned so naturally against her and her lapse is so clearly determined by her position and her position by her character. . . .*

Now I must admit that while very studious as to feelings and manners, Meilhac is devoid alike of the ethical interests displayed by Augier and Dumas *fils* and the scruples proper to a Christian and a good citizen which are observable in the comedies of Octave Feuillet. If Meilhac is moral, it is only in the least obvious and most roundabout way. He is deeply and almost

* See page 54.

invariably sceptical, ironical, irreverent. I once made a list of the things—some of them deserving of respect, others less so—which were turned daintily into ridicule in one single operetta of Meilhac's; and I found that he laughed, more particularly, at love, at maidenhood, at pastoral poetry, at Romanesque literature, at Don-Juanism, at Royalty, at the principles of the Revolution of '89, at the belief in Free Will, at science and finally at death. If he undoubtedly does love virtue, he has no idea what virtue is based on. In *Brevet Supérieur* (a failure with one scene in it of the first order), La Rochebardière, wishing to persuade Cécile to become his mistress, explains to her that a woman cannot do justice to herself save in a setting of wealth and luxury— that she must have beautiful dresses and jewels and be surrounded by all sorts of delicate little attentions and that these things need not exclude love or sincerity or goodness of heart. What is there in this picture, he pleads, to insult or hurt her? What is there in it, indeed, to be condemned? Cécile, true daughter of Paris, confesses frankly her distress of mind. " Ah ! " she cries. " It is wrong and wicked of you to talk like that. For you know, of course, that I am dying for all those things." But she adds :

HENRY MEILHAC

" All the same, I refuse, I refuse ! And yet I should find it very difficult to say why ! " And one feels that the author, also, would find it very difficult to say why.

His ideal woman is the woman lapped in luxury, either the pretty, warm-hearted little courtesan or the semi-courtesan woman of the world : the embodiment of sensual love with a background of elegance, and with touches of wit and occasionally of sentiment and tenderness. This thick-set man with the Tartar moustachios, having divested himself of all anxiety over the essential, and probably insoluble, problems of existence (or, perhaps, never having given them a thought), needed feminine forms all round him in an artificial framework, if he was to breathe and to live ; it was with his eyes and his imagination for the most part that he enjoyed them, revelling in the ingenuously guileful trickeries of the little souls encased in these forms and in the blissful gullibility of the men who fell victims to these trickeries ; perhaps it amused him sometimes to fall a half-victim to them himself in order to be able to note them with more truth and precision : a contemplative spectator of the pretty futilities and trivialities on which he sat in benignant judgment, a Cakya-Mouri of the *boulevards* in a paradise made delightful by Parisian Apsaras. And his plays seem philosophical—and doubtless are so—because the smile of Ecclesiastes, which is a simple affair and practicable for everybody (but in this case also, *il y a manière !*),* will long continue to be taken as the final word of wisdom ! . . .

To put the matter more modestly, Meilhac is essentially, and to a greater degree than people realise, the " poet " in whom the tradition of the eighteenth century has been prolonged and renewed in the nineteenth. He is, with a far greater measure of the creative faculty, of the line of Chaulieu, of Crébillon *fils*, of Parny. (An illustration occurs to me, one of a score which might be cited : the *dénouement* of *Margot*, the marriage of Margot with the gamekeeper, is it not absolutely in accordance with the philosophy of the eighteenth century ?)

The latest flower of a voluptuous civilisation, the sensuality and scepticism of Meilhac's plays are redeemed and relieved by his gentleness and by his goodness of heart. It does not do to be too much shocked by the fact that there is so much of indulgence and of real kindliness in what I shall call—because it suits me so to call it—

* *See* page 108.

HENRY MEILHAC

l'esprit de Paris. What distinguishes this *esprit de Paris* (if one is anxious to judge it benevolently) is perhaps that it presents the maximum of goodness compatible with the pursuit of pleasure ; it is an attenuation of egoism by the desire to please, the faculty of mingling tenderness or irony in what otherwise would be licentiousness pure and simple ; a refusal to be tragic, that is to say, ridiculous or wicked, whether in enjoyment or in grief ; the evolution of scepticism into a detachment of mind which, although superficial, is often compatible with the profoundest wisdom and into a gentleness which, although inactive, is on occasion the equivalent of real charity. . . .

Such is *l'esprit de Paris* in the plays of Meilhac ; and I admit that this *esprit* can be thin and foolish and displeasing enough elsewhere. If you would like to note Meilhac's spirit of gentleness, just compare *Monsieur de Pourceaugnac* with *La Vie Parisienne.* The themes are analogous : in both cases it is a grotesque figure who is in question ; but while Molière mocks at his Limousin with terrible ferocity, Meilhac treats his mystified Scandinavarian Baron so caressingly that when towards the end, he is asked : " What are you complaining about ? Have you not enjoyed yourself ? " Baron Gondremark is constrained to reply : " That is quite true, I have. What *am* I complaining about ? " He is a real good fellow, this great overgrown baby of a Gondremark. . . . So is Boisgommeux in *la Petite Marquise*. Edouard Dandrésy, in *Décoré*, is better still. He makes love to the wife of his intimate friend, but that does not prevent him from having the generous soul of a Newfoundland dog. He arrives at the rendezvous wet to the skin, having just saved an angler from drowning. He feels, as he explains to Henriette, that he would not have been worthy to possess her, had he not accomplished this deed of prowess. And little Alfred des Esquimaux in *Gotte* is of an exquisite good nature ! Marceline Lahirel has promised that she will be his when he shall have given her a proof of love which she cannot resist. Exasperated by her husband, much more than in love with Alfred, she decides to wait no longer for the proof of love for which she has stipulated, but by an unlooked-for and yet quite natural reaction the gallant youth, seized with pity for the unhappy little woman, brings home to her what a folly she is committing and advises her to be true to her fatuous spouse : " You asked me for a great proof of my love," he says. " This is the best proof I can give you." . . . In short, all Meilhac's men, or nearly all, are good ; and not one of his women are wicked, even his little cocottes having in them at the worst but a malignity of young monkeys.

It is very certain that this mingling of irreverence and gentleness, of epicurism and too soft good nature is not calculated to fortify and regenerate the soul of a people.   Good heavens, no ! But Meilhac, doubtless, did not hold that such was necessarily the purpose of the theatre.   It is equally certain, if we are anxious to compare Meilhac with others, that Augier and Dumas had more power in them and, if you like, more capacity for thought.   But, after all, the amount of thought that can be presented in the theatre will never be very great.   It is also certain that Meilhac's Paris is not the whole of Paris and that Paris is not the world.   But the comedies of Marivaux and of Musset are equally remote from containing the entire moral universe.   Let us love Meilhac as he is, since we do love him. He has infinite grace.   He has—a rare combination—with all his irony and irreverence, a *naïveté* which seems to me akin to that of La Fontaine or of Favart.   He has desolemnised comedy and made it more supple.   Almost all the new-comers,

L

the Lavedans, the Donnays, the Hermants, the Guinons, derive from him, as regards their dramatic form (in which, after all, there is nothing to hinder them from introducing lofty sentiments and a robust morality). That is a noteworthy thing about Meilhac, that he should have been able to found a school without ever having an idea of doing so and without having had a doctrine.*

[1897. Vol. X.]

* In a brief note at the end of this article Lemaître added that wherever he had written "Meilhac" the names "Meilhac and Halèvy" should be read, it being difficult to separate the two collaborators.

XIV

ODÉON : *Révottée*. A comedy in 4 Acts. By
Jules Lemaître.

I WAS rejoicing in the thought of having a
holiday this week ! It seemed to me that
this would be only right and proper. But
the editor of this journal has so much confidence
in me that he wishes me to treat of my own
comedy myself. It is his notion—perhaps quite
a wrong notion—that I know it better than anybody else. So be it, then ! I shall tell my tale
straightforwardly. The kindness of most of my
brother critics helps to make my task not too
difficult.

" Oh, God ! Grant that my child be not like
my sin, which is for ever rising up against me !
Show me, by protecting her, that Thou hast
forgiven me ! I have need of her virtue in order
to feel that I have been absolved." It seems to
me that this prayer of a " guilty mother "

expresses the initial idea out of which *Revoltée* was born.

The Comtesse de Voves, who made a loveless marriage with a man of her own world, gave birth secretly, now twenty years ago, to a child, Hélène, of whom her husband was not the father. She has had her daughter educated at a provincial convent at a distance, and she has succeeded in getting her married to a good fellow, Pierre Rousseau, a Professor of Mathematics. She has never revealed to Hélène the secret of her birth and has even shown no love for her, caring for her welfare only from afar and all too cautiously. Her excuse—if one can be found for her—is in the first place her fear lest her husband should discover her guilt, but even more that she has a son, André, from whom she would fain conceal her adventure at all costs. As it happens, André de Voves is Professor Rousseau's school-fellow and best friend. This André, brought up by his mother strictly but tenderly, is a youth of the very best heart, a paragon of affectionate devotion, with a touch of Alceste about him and a touch of Don Quixote. At the moment at which the piece opens, Mme. Hélène Rousseau, who married only to get away from the convent school, and in whom her motherless childhood

and a feeling of the hardness of her fate have
bred a spirit of bitterness and revolt, together
with the feverish yearnings that come from a
too long repression, is on the point of yielding
to the advances of a certain Jacques de Brétigny,
a sportsman and professional athlete, very
muscular, something of a fop, but quick of wit.
Now Mme. de Voves has grown to love her daughter
ardently since coming into free contact with her
and discovering how she has suffered and realising
the danger by which she is threatened ; and she
is the more resolved to face everything in order
to save her, in that, having returned to religion
at this critical period of her life, the impending
fall of her child looks to her like a retribution
for her own sin. Young André, also, is disquieted for other reasons. It is from affection
for his friend, Pierre, that he makes up his mind
to stand guard over Hélène's virtue.

Such is the situation set forth in the first Act,
which takes place in the house of the Comtesse de
Voves on a day when she is being visited by some
of her intimate friends, among others by Mme.
Herbeau, an excellent woman, somewhat eccentric in her ways but, despite an air of frivolity
about her, astute and worldly-wise ; this Mme.
Herbette, who lives alone and has independent

means, amuses herself by maintaining a literary
salon. . . .*

The second Act passes at Mme. Herbeau's, in a
little drawing-room, while a dance is in progress.
(I needed a neutral spot where all the principal
personages could meet.) Hélène and Brétigny
have taken refuge here between two waltzes.
I have tried to make their " love scene " very
typical of to-day—it is the last talk they have
before what might be called their " guilty "
talk ; it is a talk between a professional athlete
of gentlemanly bearing who is quite free from all
illusions and a young woman who, without quite
knowing what is signified by Positivism or
Darwinism or the Struggle-for-Life, yet lives in a
moral atmosphere saturated by these ideas and
who has some inkling into them and translates
them into a dry irony which comes natural to
her : a young woman, in fact, who is a kind of
intellectual and pessimistic Froufrou.

Their talk is interrupted by Mme. de Voves and
by André. The latter, troubled already by the
involuntary half-confidences by which Rousseau
has let him see how much he has suffered through

* Here in a parenthesis M. Lemaître scouts an idea which
had become current that one of the characters introduced
was a deliberate lampoon of a great writer for whom, he
protests, he has the " utmost regard and veneration."

Hélène's coldness, breaks out into violent condemnations of the young woman and, addressing Mme. de Voves, exclaims : " She is just a street-walker ! Takes after her mother, apparently ! " He proceeds to question Mme. de Voves regarding the mother who so wickedly had abandoned her daughter. Mme. de Voves, agonised by her son's cross-examination, and feeling that, alone, she can do nothing to save Hélène, makes to him in a roundabout way an avowal, which is quite explicit, of her sad secret. . . . When he has taken it in, he exclaims : " Mother, what do you want me to do ? " She replies : " Watch over Hélène—that is your duty." On which, and while Rousseau, looking utterly tired out, is taking Hélène off, André goes up to Brétigny and begs him " not to make love to Mme. Rousseau." Brétigny replies laughingly ; André tries to control himself—his blood rises and the scene closes with a challenge.

Act III.—At Pierre Rousseau's. Hélène is bored. In her heart she consents to the idea of infidelity. " What is there to stop me ? " she says to herself. " I don't believe in anything. Oh, my God, I don't believe in anything ! " . . . Rousseau comes in, accompanied by André who, before fighting the duel for his friend, has felt the need to see him again. On this occasion Rousseau has spoken out fully regarding his misery. " What you have told me," André says to him, " you must tell her. You must. Promise me ! " And, accordingly, Rousseau endeavours to win back his wife by opening his whole heart to her, the while she seeks to make light of things. He is moving and eloquent (at least I try to make him so), but he is tactless—or, rather, there is no chance for him because all her thoughts are for " the other man." The conversation is roughly broken into by a reminder of Rousseau's daily tasks—a pupil has come for his lesson—and he ends with threats. " Oh, so that's how it is ! " Hélène retorts, and she sits down at once to write to Brétigny.

At this moment Mme. de Voves enters. She has noticed how Hélène has contrived to hide the letter just written and, having made sure that all advice would be in vain, she decides to play her last card. She seizes the letter and tears it up. " But, Madame ! " exclaims Hélène. " Listen to me, you must. My son is fighting with Brétigny about you." Hélène protests vehemently against this interference on André's part. " What right has he to do so ? " she asks angrily. " What right ? You want to know ? He is fighting for

you because he is your brother, unhappy child ! "
And Mme. de Voves opens her arms to her daughter.
But Hélène does not respond. " My mother ? "
she exclaims. " No, it can't be ! " Memories of
her forlorn childhood come back to her. . . .
Mme. de Voves entreats her to break with M. de
Brétigny. Hélène will promise nothing. " Let's
forget everything," she says. " Don't make
yourself miserable over your supposed duties by
me. I shall hold you responsible for nothing,
either in the past or in the future."

Now there was, assuredly, nothing so very bold
or original about this failure of the " voice of the
blood " to speak. But we counted on this scene
a little, both M. Porel* and I. I thought that
Hélène, by the very grief she felt at feeling
nothing, and by her betrayal of it, would evoke
pity and some sympathy. . . . Well, I have to
own that the effect of this scene was less than
the effect of the preceding scenes. The fault,
obviously, is the author's. It is possible, to
begin with, that the scene is too long and that,
supposing it to be an audacious one (but audacious
only as a dramatic experiment and not beyond
the grasp of anyone), this audacity may have
been over-explained, made too articulate by the

* The manager of the theatre.

characters, and they may have seemed too conscious of it. Or, perhaps, the effect of the mother's second confession was discounted by that of her first. In my mind, the two confessions were needed for the mother's expiation to be complete, and I thought, moreover, that in form they were as different as they could be : the first indirect and involuntary, the second resolute and spoken out boldly with the energy of desperation. But perhaps I was wrong as to this. I say " perhaps " ; I would say " undoubtedly," were it not that a certain number of intelligent persons, whose good faith I have no reason to doubt, assured me that the scene pleased them as it stood.

I remember, however, that when M. Dumas was good enough two years ago to listen to my reading of the play he said to me very definitely : " Too many confessions ! There ought only to be one." " And to whom should it be made ? To the daughter or to the son ? " " To the son. And the mother should make this confession frankly, of her own accord, and without being questioned, the moment she realises that the only way to save her illegitimate daughter is to place her under the protection of her brother. And André should then go to this poor young thing and speak out to her. . . . Women are like children, sick and naughty children. They have to be roughly treated for their own welfare. Hélène must be made to feel that she is being talked to by a man, a man stronger than herself, a pure-minded man whom she can't get round." " And should André provoke Brétigny to challenge him ? " " Perhaps." " And in this case should André die ? " " Without a doubt. The death of the legitimate child will be the retribution. . . ." (The illustrious writer was thinking out for himself—without troubling his head further about *my* effort—a drama which he alone could have produced.)

The obvious way to remedy the weakness of my piece, therefore, would be to suppress the mother's confession to her daughter. Another way would be, on the contrary, to suppress the mother's confession to her son. André would be made to divine his mother's secret by himself, through certain indications. (Only it would be quite a difficult matter to imagine these indications and then to convey them with verisimilitude in such a fashion that André should put them together and that they should constitute a revelation to him. I must leave that to people who are cleverer than I.) Then André, having previously treated Hélène with some roughness, would change his tone on discovering his relationship to her; and it would be from this change in him that Mme. de Voves would divine that he knew all. . . . Such was the idea of M. Henry Lavoix, who read *Révoltée* when I offered it to the Comédie Française and who judged it with extreme severity. Strange to say, I do not resent that severity, because the piece nearly succeeded, whereas I feel I would be resenting it a little if it had failed—that is, if he had been right. It ought to be the other way about and my feeling is absurd ; but it is human.

Well, in conclusion, I shall give you the opinion of M. Ludovic Halévy. He was charming, at once very gentle and very clear-sighted, and was full of good advice. But he never stopped declaring : " This subject is too painful. . . . Oh, how painful it is ! And, then, why should André come by his death ? It is painful and it doesn't serve any purpose." " But the mother must expiate her sin," I urged. " Oh, it is expiated enough. No, look you, you must put some gaiety into it ; you must brighten it up, introduce a little happiness and laughter into it. . . . Come now, how would it be if Brétigny had a small brother who was being educated at

Condorcet and to whom Rousseau was giving lessons ? Toto, shall we call him ? Toto . . . well, it doesn't matter much what you do with him so long as we are given some relief. . . ." And so, docilely, I introduced Toto and I made a three act play of it with a happy ending. And I found that it was not as good a piece as it had been. If you are in an idle mood and disposed to take an interest in trifles, I may transcribe for you one of the scenes in which Toto appeared— that is little Georges de Brétigny, Jacques's younger brother. He came to Rousseau's house for his lesson and there met André de Voves :

André : Well, Georges, do you like your teacher ?

Georges : Yes, he is a fine chap. Besides he is full of pluck. He isn't very gay, but that's not surprising.

André : Oh, so you know why ?

Georges : Oh, well—he has a wife who is too smart for him and who is bored. I know that. Neurosis, that's what it's called nowadays. Jacques would like to have the amusing of her. I come here to get my lessons—Jacques would like to come here to give them.

André : Did you invent that joke yourself ?

Georges : No, Jacques did. Mind you, I do a

lot of useful things for Jacques. He makes me bring her tickets for the theatre and for all the places of amusement round here. And then, when my lesson's on one of her " at home " days and there aren't any visitors, I just pull up the window in old Rousseau's room without seeming to do so for any particular reason. That's a sign to Jacques, who is in the street, that she's alone and that the coast is clear for him. All quite simple, you see.

André : That's nice behaviour !

Georges : Oh, well, as she's so bored and as old Rousseau knows nothing, I'm not doing him any harm. Besides I always do everything Jacques wants me to.

André : You have a great admiration for your big brother ?

Georges : Rather ! I'm awfully keen on him. Have you ever met such a fellow ? I haven't. When I'm free——

André : Yes, when you're free—— ?

Georges : They're making me study for Saint-Cyr, but I shall fail—I can easily manage that—and then I shall live like Jacques. That's the real life, what ?

André : But, you little rascal . . . well, go on ! You interest me !

Georges : Oh, I know, you've got the old ideas. But there are very few fellows like you nowadays. What do you want a chap to do in these *fin de siècle* times, as Jacques says ? There's no more flirting to be done——

André : So you have had a try ?

Georges : Oh, yes, in a way. I'm on very good terms with Mme. de Crécy. It was Jacques introduced me to her.

André : What, Fat Liline ! You little rascal ! Do have some respect for venerable age. Why she dandled your brother on her knee when he was a baby. She might be your grandmother !

Georges (annoyed) : I beg your pardon. Perhaps I know her better than you do. Mme. de Crécy is only twenty-eight.

André : Only twenty-eight ?

Georges : Twenty-eight and three months. She proved it to me. There ! . . . Besides, she is a woman of real distinction.

Now I come to the last Act. I had to contrive an ending to the play and I found this very troublesome. The *dénouement* that was needed seemed to me André's death. A mystical aspect might be lent to such a *dénouement ;* by the shedding of the blood of her legitimate son, the mother would be expiating her abandonment of her other child. . . . But this was a very difficult thing to manage. To make the audience accept such an ending a gift for tragedy was required which I lack. Already I had disliked having to introduce a duel into my first piece !

And then I have been told that I ought to have left Hélène impenitent. But in my own mind Hélène is neither wicked nor in any way odious. Her " revolt " is natural ; and as she is intelligent and as what she revolts against is not merely her personal destiny but even more the wickedness of the world, it follows that there is at work within her a germ of philosophy which, after going through certain trials, may develop into resignation. In short, Hélène, being proud at heart, is curable—curable by the teachings of life and by the influence of some profound emotion : and she will be cured, you may be certain, the day she feels that she has made others suffer as much as, and more than, she has suffered herself. But for this her whole being needs to be shaken through and through—she needs to be driven out of her normal self by pity for a grief more poignant than her own, and raised thus, suddenly, to a standpoint whence she can see things with new eyes and in real perspective. Only the death of André would suffice for this.

But there it is! I did not dare! Or, rather, I did not know how to manage his death properly. So I resigned myself to this.

Hélène goes to see André just before the duel is to take place. She complains that she, " a woman of the time," is being officiously dragged by him into the situation of a stage heroine. . . . André, very grave, replies to her : " What do you want to bring home to me ? That I have acted thus without your consent ? But it is without your consent, also, that there is a moral law, a solidarity of honour between the members of the same family, ties of affection stronger than all else, feelings held to be sacred, feelings which conform with an eternal order of things and which one obeys sometimes without asking what the consequences may be. It is only in such moments that one is really worth anything. . . ." And he tells her all he knows—frankly but tenderly. Hélène has begun to bow her head a little, touched by the element of moral beauty and greatness in his words. Grace is coming to her— quite swiftly. But André has scarcely left the spot when Rousseau appears. He suspects the cause of the duel. He is in defiant mood, almost menacing. Mme. de Voves stops him from speaking, for there must be an end to this, and the scene comes to nothing. André now is brought in, dangerously wounded. While all press round him, Hélène advances beseechingly towards Mme. de Voves and begins : " Mother, forgive me ! " " No, you have cost me too much ! " is the reply. Hélène hesitates a moment, seeking some support in her distress. But her natural support is, after all, her husband still : " Pierre ! she rejects me ! Pierre, I beg of you—— ! " " No, Hélène, my heart is too heavy and you have done me too much harm." At this moment the wounded man calls to her ; she grasps the hand he has stretched out to her and he reconciles her with her husband and with his mother. " I have given her back to you both," he cries. " I am happy ! "

A very mediocre Act, this last one, as you see. Now I have thought of a better ending, and one in which André need not die. . . . But it is too late.

The piece was considered to have been very well acted. I publicly thank my interpreters, all of them, and without entering into details as to their respective merits. For if their talents are perhaps a little unequal, I owe equal gratitude to them all.

JULES LEMAÎTRE

Evil is often spoken of journalists and men of letters. It is declared that we do not show much affection for each other and that we are not free from selfishness and malice. Now, quite apart from those who are my friends and who have judged me with a sympathy which I reciprocate, the majority have dealt with me in a spirit of perfect loyalty and justice which does honour, it seems to me, to our confraternity ; can it be that, when all is taken into account, we are better fellows than the *bourgeois* ? My thanks, there-fore, to almost all my colleagues and from the bottom of my heart !

[15th April, 1889. Vol. IV.]

XV

COMÉDIE FRANÇAISE : *Mariage Blanc*. A Play in 3 Acts. By Jules Lemaître.

I SHALL begin by warning you to regard as null and void the articles on *Mariage Blanc* which have already appeared, even those which have not been too hard on me—even, if you like, the one written by my admirable *confrère* Henry Fouquier, who has contrived to put forward the best possible defence of my piece merely by the way in which he has expounded it.

I know, of course, that all those hostile notices carry weight and that the damage done to me thereby must be considerable. But really they should not count. For all the articles upon the *première* were written after the *répétition générale* and under the force of the impressions then received. In other words, the work was publicly judged before it belonged to the public and, what is more serious, before it had been given its final form.

THEATRICAL IMPRESSIONS

It was with the play of Thursday that the critics dealt : now the play of Friday was in reality another play, quite different from the one they had heard, and acted in quite a different way.

Some of the critics betrayed themselves ingenuously. On Thursday there was an open window in *Mariage Blanc*. On Friday we closed it. But certain absent-minded critics, whom I shall not name, have left it open.

I am stating facts, not recriminating. My brother critics have but done in this case what I myself may have done more than once. I am merely twitting them with their lapse and lodging an appeal with my Monday readers and the public—that is all ; when the public and my Monday readers shall have pronounced their verdict there shall be no further appeal, I promise you—not even to Posterity !

It is the fact, however, that *Mariage Blanc* in its penultimate form astonished and afflicted many good people and others as well.

And yet it seemed to me and, despite everything, seems to me still, that the idea of the piece was so simple, so natural, so easily understood ; I will even add so strictly moral !

Comte Jacques de Thièvres is an idler who is bored, a *viveur* grown disgusted with life, still interested in things, however, and a bit of a dilettante, not without brains, not corrupted, rather a good fellow at heart than otherwise. He meets at Mentone a quite young girl suffering from consumption, very gentle, very sweet, Simone Aubert. He discovers that her one great misery lies in the thought that she is going to die without having lived her life like other women. One day he hears her declare : " Most of my friends are married. The others all have men fond of them and making love to them. No one has ever made love to me. I shall never know what it is to be loved and to marry and to become a mother." On this, Jacques is set thinking : " I am bored, I am on the look-out for something that makes life worth living. Well, here is something. Why not give to this poor little girl the happiness she never hopes to have ? Why not give her the illusion of living that woman's life, that illusion of being loved ? " . . . And he asks for Simone's hand in marriage. He expresses him- self touchingly and reassuringly to her mother, giving his reasons : " I do not forget that it is an invalid you will be confiding to my care and this child who will be leaving your arms will remain a child still in mine. A great desire has come to me to be with her, to watch over her always.

Now, only marriage can enable me to do this. What I ask, in fact, is the right to live with her as if I were her elder brother. Nothing can be purer than this tender feeling."

He is speaking the truth and the mother realises it. And, therefore, after a moment's doubt and hesitation, seeing that Simone is fond of Jacques and that this " white marriage " may, in truth, bring her an illusory happiness and comfort, whereas a refusal would doubtless kill her, she accedes to the Count's request.

All would go well, and the story would be quite edifying, were it not that Simone has a sister—a half-sister, that is to say—Marthe, strong and full-blooded, but sad, and just a little neglected by the mother.

Jacques, who has had enough, and more than enough, to do with women and who is entirely preoccupied with the gracious and kindly action he has in view, has taken no notice of this other girl, despite her good looks. But Marthe has persuaded herself that it is on her account he frequents the house. Simone herself at first took the same view. " For whom else would he come ? " she said to her sister. " He is in love with you, I'm sure. I shall ask him and find out." And Marthe takes flight, tremulous with hope. When she returns, Simone and Jacques are engaged ! . . . And now, poor Marthe, believing that Simone has played her false, is scarcely able to keep back her anger and despair. She does restrain herself, however, seized by a sudden feeling of pity, for Simone is overcome and faints. Marthe is not bad at heart—not yet, at least. Indeed, there are no really bad people in my play.

And so Jacques marries his little invalid. Simone is happy. Jacques treats her like a child, as he promised to do ; she gets better and seems to take on new life. Marthe, more than ever in love with Jacques, looks on with bitterness at this joy of which she feels she has been robbed. It must be admitted that Simone has not been absolutely loyal and that she has acted in all this with a little of the terrible and yet excusable egoism of those who suffer. . . . At last, one day when Simone has been talking a little too imprudently about her bliss, Marthe, maddened by jealousy, gives full vent to her feelings, and there is a dreadful scene in which she accuses Simone of treachery. Simone, horror-stricken, has a choking fit ; Jacques carries her to her bed and, while her mother cares for her, he returns to Marthe, with whom he remonstrates sternly.

He begins well enough : " You know that what

you have just done is atrocious." But alas !
Jacques is no saint. Before him he has this
handsome young girl torn with love for him,
entreating him to forgive her and promising him
that she will go away at once—but not until she
has seen him once more to say good-bye.
Jacques ought to leave her but he does not. He
remains, touched in spite of himself by this
display of passion. He says more or less what
he ought to say, but he is wrong to pick up a
shawl which Marthe has dropped and to replace
it on her shoulders, looking her in the eyes, and
above all to consent to that last meeting for
which she pleads.

His consent is out of pity chiefly and without
actual thought of wrong, but that is not quite all.
It is a summer evening and something of the
voluptuary in him reawakes. " Until to-night,
then ! " he ends by saying, as though to get rid
of her. . . . But Simone, who has recovered and
who has grown disquieted over her husband's
absence, has heard these last words, has seen the
incident of the shawl and seen Marthe seize
Jacques's hands as though to kiss them, and she
has fallen to the ground, dead, like a flower
before the scythe.

And the moral of the story is that a sensualist

with an inquiring mind must always find it very difficult to become a really good man ; that what " does for " Jacques is the fact that he undertakes an act of charity which is in its nature evangelistic without himself having the genuinely evangelistic spirit ; that a former Don Juan, or even a man of dilettante temperament, will only have within him a very small fraction of the makings of a Saint Vincent de Paul ; that one can do a great deal of harm by doing good in too ingenious and too resourceful a fashion and with too great self-complacency—if that can be called doing good at all ; that true goodness, simple disinterested goodness, is incompatible with the detached attitude of a man for whom the world is, above all, a spectacle ; that—well, that is as much as I know, but I should like to borrow from my good Dr. Doliveux some of his remarks : " There is something too artfully concocted, a basis of egoistic curiosity, in your act of charity . . . and it is possible that the thing may not end well. You an't do what you say without telling lies from morning till night and from night till morning. . . . To play with this child, who is so absolutely innocent, the comedy which you have in mind seems to me an offence against nature and against love, and I fear lest love and nature may avenge themselves. . . ." Only the good doctor seems to me a trifle too severe. The co-existence of dilettantism with real goodness does not seem to me so impossible. Note, moreover, that in the course of the drama Jacques' feeling of curiosity goes more and more into the background, that his tender regard for Simone becomes more deep and sincere, and that if she dies through his action, after he has brought her comfort and increased health, it is by a fatality which he could not possibly foresee. His momentary lapse has terrible consequences but in itself is excusable enough. If Jacques had had no sister-in-law, he would have felt that he had done a wonderfully fine thing, and that is the fact. And in this case there would have been no moral to my story and *Mariage Blanc* would be merely a " pretty play " causing people to reflect now and again on charity and dilettantism. Nothing more.

What I have detailed above is the gist of the play in its final form, as it was softened ; but it is not against this, I say again, that the critics have directed their arguments.

It is possible, however, that I have been misguided and in two ways.

My first mistake was to believe that there was

nothing extraordinary about Jacques de Thièvres' idea, and that his feelings and his conduct were very easy to understand. But I could not well believe otherwise for I quite well remember cherishing Jacques's dream myself twelve or fifteen years ago. It came to me quite spontaneously apropos of a young girl whom I met in a *pension de famille* in which I took my meals. No doubt it was merely a dream, a thing to be put into verse (I wrote verse in those days and if, by some strange chance, you should know my first book, you will find in it a sonnet entitled " Phthisica ") ; but really this dream has never seemed to me so absurd or so impracticable. Least of all did it seem to me that it could be deemed immoral. I certainly brought to this meditated act of kindness a little of the self-consciousness and self-complacency shown by Jacques, but if it seemed to me a charming thing to do, it was on the understanding, first and foremost, that it should remain chaste. And it seemed to me later that a man of forty or forty-five who should have lived through a lot and become rather weary, but not perverted, would be the kind of man most capable of keeping to this intention of absolute chastity.

Imagine my astonishment when I saw Jacques

accused of sadism. This accusation seems to me the outcome of the over-wrought mental condition and pedantic immorality of some of the spectators.

My second mistake was in thinking that the idea of the death was not unbearably sad. The fact is that for a long time past, and in accordance with the teachings of philosophers and saints, this idea is mixed up in my mind with almost all other ideas. I imagined quite frankly that the spectacle of a young invalid who is really happy during more than half the piece and who is not struck down by the fatal but swift blow until the end, would be tinged by a very gentle kind of sadness, a sadness in no way torturing. Apparently I was wrong. One critic having accused me of *vampirisme*, another, of equal standing, accused me of *cruellisme*.

In short, I thought I was producing a drama which was clear and intelligible and it has been judged obscure ; I thought I was producing a drama full of tenderness and it is condemned for ferocity.

Only, I repeat, what has been called ferocious and obscure was not the version submitted to the public on the " first night " ; it was an earlier version which was held to have been abolished.

JULES LEMAÎTRE

For there were three successive versions of *Mariage Blanc*, and this without the text having been altered. There was merely a little less text in the second version than in the first, and much less in the third than in the second. *Voilà tout!*

M. Jules Clarétie, during the rehearsals, amused himself thinking out titles for the piece. He invented some which were ingenious or funny. Here are three : *On ne badine pas avec la mort ;* or *Trois Blondes* (because of the blonde hair of Mmes. Reichenberg, Pierson and Marsy) ; or *Le Bon Curieux*. These titles seemed to me quite well fitted to be applied to the three dwindling manuscripts of *Mariage Blanc*.

1°. *On ne badine pas avec la mort.* That is the text of the play which was read to the Committee. In this text Jacques was a dilettante given somewhat to expounding his ideas at length and obviously pleased with his dilettantism. Marthe was quite frankly a criminal. She deliberately opened a window behind her sister's back to kill her. And Jacques, at first very sincerely shocked, went so far, at the end of a long scene, as to kiss her on the mouth (ten minutes after kissing Simone) and as to suggest a meeting with her himself for the evening at the bottom of the garden. All this was very carefully worked up to, mind, and was less odious than it will seem to you : there was a series of emotional scenes and incidents, involving trials for the senses, defeat for the will. In fact, the play was a tragedy, of a very pale hue undoubtedly, for my humble Marthe is far removed in every way, and even in her wicked acts, from a Hermione or a Roxane or a Phèdre ; but a tragedy it was.

2°. *Trois Blondes*. This was the text used in the *répétition générale*, the text which displeased some persons so much. And yet we had spent a whole month eliminating, toning down, softening, haunted as we were by the questions : " How will the public take that ? How much can it stand ? " And it is curious how, throughout the business of rehearsing, one pictures the public in the guise of a portentous old gentleman, very virtuous, very severe, of very limited intelligence, very easy to shock, and at the same time very larky and very keenly on the look-out for improprieties, so that one goes through the entire text, phrase by phrase, for fear of leaving anything in it that could be read in a double sense. . . . In this second text, Marthe did not open the window of deliberate purpose : she opened it thoughtlessly and because she felt the room too hot. Jacques, in the last scene, did not kiss her on the mouth ; he merely acquiesced in regard to the rendezvous which the excited girl suggested, in order to make an end to a painful scene. His whole crime was to listen too long and to seem to forget his agonised wife just for a moment. You see the attenuations already made. But the idea of the death continued to cast its shadows over the whole piece. Then Jacques, a very good fellow in Act II, much more to be pitied than to blame in Act III, was still allowed in Act I to give expression to ideas of a somewhat frigid dilettantism—and to excess. It was not understood that Jacques is one of those people who are better than their words—and than some of their actions—and who, by reason of this, are unable to bring their good deeds to completion. Therefore it was necessary to tone down Jacques de Thièvres still more and make him more sympathetic.

3°. *Le bon Curieux*. This is the text of the First Night. We had spent our afternoon improving Jacques's character, brightening up Simone, whitewashing Marthe, cutting out medical details and erasing the words " death " and " dying " wherever they could be erased. . . . At this point I can hear someone say : " In short, every conceivable cowardice ! But, my good

sir, do you not stand up for your own ideas ? "
I shall reply to this another time. . . . In this
third text, the time of Simone's death is not
indicated—the audience may hope that she will
continue to live ; Jacques no longer airs his
disquieting ideas ; Marthe does not open the
window ; Jacques in the last scene remains cen-
sorious of her, and does not look at her with too
much interest in his eyes, and his whole fault is
reduced to his momentary feeling of disturbance
caused by the proximity of this beautiful, over-
wrought young girl. . . . It is still his dilettante
temperament which spoils his kind action and
kills Simone—but much less directly. The
drama retains some of its meaning but it is less
clear. On the other hand, it may seem more
moving in this form.

And now what am I to say to you about my
interpreters ? I have not enough time at my
disposal to praise them as I should like and I am
too tired to seek the fine adjectives which are
called for by their talent. You will assuredly
have admired Mlle. Reichenberg's adorable grace
and her perfection, so simple and so living, as
Simone ; the depth of emotion in the accents of
Mme. Blanche as Mme. Hubert ; the generous and

superb beauty and fire of Mlle. Marsy as Marthe ; and the verve and cordiality of M. Laroche as Dr. Doliveux.

As for M. Frédéric Febvre—to him I shall come back. All I can say to you to-day is that he staged my piece with a fertility of expressive and picturesque invention, with a feeling for elegance and at the same time for truth, and with an abundance of ideas, at which I have marvelled ; in fact, in mounting the play in this way, he has really been my collaborator ; and within a few hours, between the *répétition générale* and the first performance, he wrought the miracle of entirely transforming the air and tone of Jacques and of making quite another person of him from top to toe. He liked my piece and believed in it ; he really carried it on his robust shoulders at its first performance. I cherish a profound feeling of gratitude towards him and I hope to express it to him better some other time.*

⌊23rd March, 1891. Vol. VI.⌋

* In Mr. A. B. Walkley's " Playhouse Impressions " will be found an admirable criticism of *Mariage Blanc*.   F.W.

XVI

GYMNASE : *l'Age Difficile*, a Comedy in three
Acts, by Jules Lemaître.

THE literature of personal revelations is
condemned, and with reason, by persons
of fastidious minds. But the public
likes it, so what is one to do? The public gives
proofs daily of this taste and perhaps authors
who are weak enough to minister to it may
therefore be excused. Moreover, a man need
not be in the first rank of writers to win forgiveness for his disclosures; after all, what
we still enjoy in Marmontel, a mediocrity,
are his familiar *Mémoires*. These thoughts
encourage me to recount to you quite simply
how I conceived the theme, the character and
the plot of *l'Age Difficile*. And I have another
excuse: there is at least one individual to whom
I shall be giving pleasure, namely, M. Alfred
Binet, of the Sorbonne, who began last
year that quaint investigation of his into " the

psychology of dramatic authors," great authors and small, and into the mysterious workings of their brain, strong or weak. Give me, then, your absolution once again for my sin of *auto-reportage* !

" *Je ne songeais pas à Rose . . .*"—I mean I was not thinking of M. Coquelin when I was invited to write a comedy in which he should take the principal rôle. I said to myself naturally : " Let us take a subject from M. Coquelin's own personality (his artistic personality, of course), from what we know of his talent, of his aptitudes, and even of his secret aspirations. The great comedian is no longer in the flower of his first youth ; he is a great comic actor, but he knows also how to interpret emotions of tenderness and grief ; he has always plumed himself thereon, and his leanings in this direction are stronger than ever. . . . What can his age be ? About fifty, I imagine. Let us, then, look about for *une aventure morale** conceivable for a man of fifty."

There is, of course, such a situation as that

---

* It would be stupid to translate this : " a moral adventure " ; and one finds it difficult to think of any English equivalent. An English playwright would have talked probably of a dramatic situation or problem or predicament or experience. F.W.

of Arnolphe in *l'Ecole des Femmes*, of Max de Simiers in *La Souris*, etc., etc., but it has been presented so often that it would certainly seem *banal*. . . . Supposing we make Coquelin a little older ? The case of the man of sixty is even more interesting, don't you think, and, I will not say never, but less completely, exploited ? We shall avoid, of course, such a situation as that of old Danville in *l'Ecole des Vieillards*, which is really but that of Arnolphe exaggerated. Besides, I feel that, in spite of myself, I should be severe to the point of injustice (a kind of injustice which the public would not understand) on a sexagenarian in love. We must look for something of a more general order.

And as when one sets to work imagining one always begins at once to call up memories, and as the memories are always connected with ourselves, the plot I was in search of evolved gradually out of a thought which is often in my mind and which is one of the fruits of my individual experience. . . .

> " Vennent les ans !   J'aspire à cet âge sauveur
> Où mon sang coulera plus sage dans mes veines . . .
> Et vous, oh ! quel poignard de ma poitrine ôté,
> Femmes ! quand de l'amour il n'y sera plus traces,
> Et qu' enfin je pourrai ne voir dans la beauté
> Que le dépot en vous du moule pur des races ! "

THEATRICAL IMPRESSIONS

So speaks Sully-Prudhomme in *les Solitudes*. I myself have long felt the conviction that my old age, if I have one, and provided it be not too heavily weighted with physical complaints, will be far and away the happiest time of my life, and it is for that period I store up my pleasantest dreams.* But I foresee also that in order to arrive at this blissful condition of detachment and security and well-being and peace,

(" Repose toi, mon âme, en ce dernier asile,
Ainsi qu'un voyageur qui, le cœur plein d'espoir,
S'assied, avant d'entrer, aux portes de la ville
Et respire un moment l'air embaumé du soir.")

there must be a bad crossing to get over, especially for those whom the phases of a normal life and an almost unceasing succession of daily tasks shall not have borne along to the threshold of old age. For these, and for even the best among them, the beginning of the sixties must be the age which is pre-eminently " difficult," the age at which they find themselves most exposed to mistakes and sufferings—ignoble or

---

* These dreams, one is sorry to know, were not to be realised. Jules Lemaître, who was born in April, 1853, died on August 5, 1914. For some years previously, he had been all too " heavily weighted with physical complaints." He had his books, however, and some devoted friends to comfort him.—F. W.

generous according to the measure of their minds. . . .

And so my chief character begins to take shape. I make him rich and cultivated so that he may have the more time and capacity for thought ; and good, because I want to like him and because, after all, the good are just as interesting as the others ; in his sixtieth year and an old bachelor ; not, however, an old bachelor from selfishness and calculation, but because of an unhappy love-affair in his youth.

The perils and the unhappiness of solitude for an elderly man have been foreseen by him, and he has wished to guard himself against them. He has sought and has found pasturage for his heart. Ten years ago he adopted a little orphan, a niece of his, and he has brought her up and married her off to a good fellow whom he has taken into partnership in his business. Jeanne has children ; he adores them just as he adores their mother ; he rejoices in this dual parentage. He is, moreover, a captain of industry, he works hard and he looks after the interests of his men. He believes he has escaped alike the misery of solitude and the danger and dishonour of uselessness and vicious idleness. " Yes," he will explain to one of his friends, " when one has spent one's life outside the normal lines of existence, whether like you, who have never taken marriage and fatherhood seriously, or like myself, who have remained celibate, one feels at a loss after fifty." And he will proceed : " At our age, when one has no family of one's own, one must contrive to acquire one. One must find a child to grow fond of, and I have had the happiness to find Jeanne. One must get to like people, or at least to take an interest in them—which I find easier than liking them. You know what I have done for my workmen. . . ."

Here we have the primary idea of the piece. But there is a supplementary one. In order to grow old happily, it is not enough to love, it is necessary to love disinterestedly. " At our age," someone else will say to my sexagenarian, " we have to love without exacting, or even wanting, to be loved equally in return. . . . Our love must not be a selfish love—we must leave that to the young. . . ." And the whole play will be a demonstration of the truth of this.

My man—I call him Chambray—oppresses his niece and her husband, Jeanne and Pierre Martigny, with his imperious and tyrannical affection. I don't want this tyranny to seem odious, and that is why I not only make it unconscious but I explain it by Chambray's character and antecedents : he was at one time an explorer, he has always been accustomed to command, he is a man of action and energy. The relationship of these three, although they are fond of each other, is none the less unnatural —it cannot last. But how will its unnaturalness assert itself ? How will the egotism underlying Chambray's deep affection become manifest ? How will his mistake react against himself ?

The solution is very simple. This little household which he has grown to love so well, he will endanger its happiness by the nature of his love. Pierre, ill at ease and unhappy at his own fireside, with Chambray for ever interposing between him and his wife, between him and his children, will take a mistress. That is inevitable. But what kind of mistress ?

Will it be a regular *cocotte* ? Or a little *bourgeoise*, half sentimental, half depraved ? No, we have seen so many of these types. Besides, it is essential that Pierre's lapse shall be reduced to a minimum so that his wife may not find it too difficult later to forgive him : her forgiveness of him is to involve Chambray's punishment. The temptress must come and seek out Pierre, she must make the advances ; it must be she who shall seduce him. Therefore, she must be a bit of a bad lot. And it will be desirable to make Pierre shy and awkward—this will help to explain why he has not been better able to stand up against his wife's masterful uncle and hold his own. . . . " It is all this cursed shyness ! " he will exclaim somewhere in the play : " It has always been impossible for me to pass from thought to action. If anyone is looking on, I am afraid to make a move. . . . It is miserable to be like that ! . . ."

What sort of young person, then, is this temptress—Yoyo, as I shall call her—to be ? She shall be just a non-moral creature of the type of to-day, neurotic, a morphiamaniac, etc., and dressed accordingly. . . . I shall emphasise her *coquinerie* and I shall give her a husband, who shall be her partner in vice, her " protector." This husband, whom I shall call M. de Montaille, will be an amusing foil to her ; but, apart from that—it suddenly occurs to me—he can be made to help on the action ; I shall make him behave like a famous husband of whom I used to hear, who was in the habit of selling art curios at a high price to his wife's lovers. And it will be the sight of some antique which has been delivered at the Martignys' home that will arouse Jeanne's suspicions as to poor foolish Pierre's infidelity.

Yes, but how to explain the circumstance that such a pair as Yoyo and her husband should be in friendly touch with the Martignys? I shall give Yoyo a father—whom I shall call Vaneuse—and this father will have been a friend from childhood's days of old Chambray. Vaneuse will serve, moreover, to illustrate the other way, the ignoble way, of crossing the threshold of the " difficult age." He and his daughter and her husband will make a pretty trio of low-down rogues. . . .

Thus Pierre Martigny will allow himself to be led astray by Yoyo, falling an easy prey to her. When Jeanne hears of this, Chambray does his utmost to intensify the grief and anger of his niece and to separate her from her husband, thinking he will have her all to himself again. For the affection of this old man for his niece is one of those affections—entirely chaste but profoundly jealous—which make certain fathers fade away and die or commit suicide (such suicides have been known) when their daughters have married and left them. But Jeanne and Pierre, being young and wholesome and in love with each other, will end by coming together again in spite of Chambray : they will open out their hearts to each other and forgive each other. And now Pierre, in one of those outbursts to which timid men are prone, will give Chambray a piece of his mind and will carry Jeanne off with him, right out of the house, and Chambray will find himself abandoned and solitary. . . . This will be the end of the second Act. About all this part of the play I am not bothered much. I feel almost sure I shall acquit myself creditably with it, as I have less trouble over the expression of my feelings and ideas than over the invention of facts. But what is to come now ?

Chambray, through his own fault and in punishment for having been selfish in his love, has been thrown into the state of isolation which he feared so much. Will he succumb to the evil temptations which attend it and sink to the hideous condition of a Vaneuse ? No, I want to save him from that, for he deserves to be saved. How shall I set about it ?

It is necessary at this point to show that Chambray is not only a good man but certainly has it in him to become better still ; that his affection for Jeanne and Pierre is of the kind that withstands everything and that is susceptible of purification. It was necessary to imagine something that would prove him capable of loving unselfishly and this by facing risks for those he loves—and without telling them and at the very moment when he believes them to be ungrateful and when he imagines he hates them and his heart is full of bitterness. . . . I have it ! I shall bring back the rascally Montaille. He shall come and say to Chambray, with some circumlocutions : " I am under the regrettable necessity of challenging your nephew to a duel. I am a formidable swordsman. It is very sad for your niece. But you know about my financial embarrassments. . . . An arrangement might be come to if you liked." Upon which, Chambray will denounce Montaille as the scoundrel he is and will take on the affair himself. This scene will have the additional advantage of restoring to Chambray the sympathy of the public.

Chambray's paternal instincts continue thus to work in his breast without his realising it, and in an entirely disinterested way. From this point on, I feel at ease in my mind about the *dénouement* up to which I am working. But this *dénouement* cannot come just yet, nor can it be reached through the efforts of Jeanne and her husband, for Chambray's wound is a very grave one. And, then, it is fitting, it accords with the truth, that after the sufferings of the " difficult age," he should have to cope with its temptations. . . . The temptress ? She is easily found—she shall be Yoyo herself. This forlorn (and rich) sexagenarian is marked out to be her quarry.

Bnt how to make them meet ? She cannot present herself at his house all at once after what has happened. So it must be Vaneuse, her father, Chambray's old friend, who will introduce them and act as his daughter's herald. . . . . Yoyo will come and confide to Chambray her grief and penitence. And I think I know what will pass between them.

Chambray will seem lost, but I repeat he is worthy of being saved and he carries within him that which will save him. Only, he needs some kind of shock which will make him look into his own heart and see things clearly—which will constrain him, so to speak, to find his soul again. The steps taken by Jeanne and Pierre would not suffice ; I shall prove this by some tactless intervention on the part of Pierre, which will only appear to Chambray to show that these two whom he loves can perfectly well do without him. . . . What, then, will be his saving ?

I may remind you that if Chambray has remained unmarried, it is not his own fault. As he himself remarks, at some point : " The real thing is to marry at twenty-five and to be a grandfather at fifty." And this, if you like, may be regarded as the third moral of the piece. He will go on to say : " As a father and grand-father, I should have been stood by. Then, having known happiness, I should not at this turning-point of my life have had this yearning for love which has made life unbearable for me." It would have been a delight to him to be a father and a grandfather ; it was a misunder-standing that had prevented his marriage with the young girl whom he loved. He deserved, therefore, to win back by an effort and in a round-about way the sensations and the joys of normal old age. . . . Why should they not be brought to him by that early love of his ? Yes, it shall be so. I shall bring back to him the girl whom forty years ago he was unable to marry, an elderly woman now, a widow, who has had her sorrows in life, alone now herself also, and faithful, throughout everything, to her first love. It is she who will save her old friend and who will press Jeanne and Pierre and their little ones back into his arms and who will teach him what he has begun to divine : how to love at sixty. And this old love of his, who will give me my *dénouement*, will have helped me also with the presentation of the idea of the play : Jeanne, questioned by her in the first Act, will have told her all that the audience needs to know in advance.

And now all I have to do is to write the play !

[Vol. IX]

XVII

COMÉDIE-FRANÇAISE : *Œdipe roi*, Tragedy of Sophocles. Translation by Jules Lacroix.

THE Comédie-Française has revived *Œdipe Roi*. Let us be grateful. It is a magnificent spectacle and the rendering of the play, taken as a whole, is entirely worthy of our leading theatre. There is a joy—a joy with just a touch of sadness in it—in feeling ourselves to be still in communion, across the twenty-three centuries which intervene, with the most cherished and most revered of our intellectual ancestors. Not that this joy has been, for me, free from all anxiety. I shall tell you presently of my doubts and discomforts. I shall begin, however, by telling you of my pleasure.

A pleasure of curiosity and a pleasure of veneration, to begin with. Do what we may, we cannot forget that the spectacle set forth before our eyes was unfolded first before the

noblest and most intelligent of ancient races
and that these same words we are hearing moved
the souls of the conquerors of Marathon and
of Salamis.   And (it is a touching thought)
this makes *us* eager to be moved also !   For the
rest, we are aware that these performances,
which were at once operas and tragedies and
even ballets, wherein all the arts—music, poetry,
dancing, painting, sculpture—conspired together
to form a representation of human life that
should have a sovereign character of beauty—
these pastimes which were enacted beneath
the blue sky, beside the blue sea, in a theatre
in which ten thousand spectators found room
upon the tiers hewed out of the virgin rock—
must have been of a majesty and splendour
incomparable.   Then we carry within us visions
of the art of Greece, memories of the friezes
of the Parthenon ; we dream of a form of poetry
at once scholarly and spontaneous, very
harmonious and very sincere, ancient and yet
ever young.   And as we hope to find something
of all that upon these narrow boards, under
this artificial light, behind this scholarly and
conscientious French translation, we succeed,
in truth, in doing so.   It is enough for us that
the scenery shows a bit of the Madeleine, that

the costumes fall in heavy folds, that the actors are very deliberate and ample in their gestures, and that they play their part with conviction, gravity and reverence, for it to be possible for us to believe we are back in those times all aglow with gladness. . . . Pericles himself might be of our family.

Another pleasure to be derived from *Œdipus Tyrannus* is that which we get from a piece which has been very well contrived, from the artifices or the craftsmanship of a d'Ennéry or a Sardou. And the pleasure is doubled in this instance by a certain astonishment—one cannot get over the fact that they were able " to turn out such good work " more than two thousand years ago ! On the last occasion on which *Œdipus Tyrannus* was revived, it was on this head above all that the critics became ecstatic.

And, indeed, the series of partial discoveries by which Œdipus attains to complete knowledge of the horrible truth is conducted and graduated with an ability and a sureness of touch which are marvellous. I shall point out merely (and the fact is all to our credit) that this was not realised until our own time. This tragedy seemed to Corneille somewhat childish in its simplicity, and Voltaire saw in it only a work which was formless and barbarous. And they remodelled it—and " perfected " it, alas !

To their mind Sophocles had been maladroit twice over : first in allowing us to foresee from the beginning the *dénouement* of the drama ; then in prolonging far beyond all probability the persistent doubts of Œdipus and his resistance against the evidence. They did not perceive that this obstinacy on the King's part, this refusal to see what is clear as the day, was, here, profound and poignant in its truth. And they did not suspect either that in measuring out the truth to us in their perfected versions of the play, so that we might not forestall the son of Laïus in his investigation, they themselves were violating one of the essential rules of dramatic art. This rule is that in the theatre the poet must always let us into the secret. It is not we whom he must surprise, but the characters in his play. As Diderot said excellently, one must always bring things home to the *dramatis personæ*, not to the spectators. . . . The poet by withholding from me his secret affords me a moment's surprise ; by taking me into his confidence he might have kept me in prolonged suspense. This law, which was long in being established (for it could only be the

SOPHOCLES

fruit of long experience) finds in *Œdipus Tyrannus* its earliest and most striking exemplification. And, strange to note, if Sophocles has here given us a " well-made play," it is precisely because the law in question has been followed, because the poet has placed us *au courant* with things frankly and from the start. This enabled him, in fact, to have regard only for his hero, to take account only of *his* state of mind, ignoring ours. If he had paid attention to ours, if he had been afraid of telling us too much, it would have been impossible for him to link up his revelations in the way he has done, and thus to display in the conduct of his drama the mastery which is so praised to-day.

Let us enter into details and put this to the test. It is in the second scene of the play that the soothsayer Tiresias makes it clear that it is Œdipus who has killed Laïus : " . . . This man whom you are seeking, this murderer whom you curse, he is here. He passes for a stranger, but he will learn that Thebes is his Country and he will not have cause to rejoice therefor. Blind and a beggar, leaning on a staff, he will journey into foreign lands, for he will be the brother of his children, the son of his wife, the assassin of his father."

THEATRICAL IMPRESSIONS

" We have nothing more to learn," remarked Voltaire : " and behold, the piece completely finished ! " But not for Œdipus ! So great and so terrible a truth could not enter instantly into his mind. The declaration made by Tiresias troubles and excites him without convincing him. And now begins a series of ill-directed questionings, which assuredly add nothing to what we know of the past of Œdipus, but which enlighten us much regarding what a man may suffer. The King of Thebes starts when he hears the soothsayer's accusations. He believes Tiresias to have been bribed by Creon, to whom he journeys to pick a senseless quarrel. Then he questions Jocasta. The Queen, to reassure him and to show the vanity of predictions, tells him how it had been prophesied that her son would be the assassin of Laïus and how, in order to avert this, she had exposed her son on Mount Cithœron. Œdipus, for his part, recalls how at Corinth a drunken man called him a foundling ; how an oracle had predicted that he would kill his father and enter his mother's bed ; how he had left Corinth in order to escape this dreadful destiny ; and finally how he had killed a man who might be Laïus.

" And behold the piece completed a second

time ! " exclaimed Voltaire. " This Œdipus must be an idiot not to understand."

A messenger now comes to announce to Œdipus that Polybus is dead, adding, in order to console him, that Polybus was not his father : this man-servant it was who, while minding the flocks on Mount Cithœron, received Œdipus as a small child from the hands of a shepherd in the service of Laïus. The said shepherd is sent for, and he declares that the child has been consigned to him by Jocasta.

" The third *dénouement*," says Voltaire : " the third conclusion, identical with the two previous ones. What an ill-constructed piece ! "

What a strange idea, rather, this idea of Voltaire's. When we read the tragedy of Sophocles, is it to find out who has killed Laïus and who are the parents of Œdipus ? We have long known all about that. What constitutes the dramatic power of *Œdipus Tyrannus* is just the way in which we are informed of what Œdipus ignores or would fain ignore : the last word in the long development comes as a thunderclap for him only alone, and not for us. What kindles and excites our curiosity and compassion from scene to scene is the sight of this luckless man, driven to his ruin by a superior power, alternately seeking and rejecting desperately the clue to his fate : the sight of him tearing asunder, by his act but against his own will, the veil which hangs before his eyes. We do not ask : " What, then, is this mystery ? " but : " How will he pierce through it ? " And this second question is of a very different interest from the first. How will he learn who he is and whence he comes ? By what progression of anxieties, of lights dubious for him alone, and through what surprises, what mental conflicts and moods of indignation, will he arrive at the solution of this problem which lures and terrifies him ? That is what I find in the work of Sophocles. And this is the veritable pleasure—the pleasure which endures and which renews itself. The other (that of surprise) is a pleasure of an hour, a pleasure which dies after the first reading of the play or the first seeing of it, and which is not to be felt again. To see the characters in a play exciting themselves affords me the more pleasure in that I know better than they whither the poet is taking them. It is a case of one's intelligence being enhanced by foreknowledge : one of God's own pleasures, if you please !

And now for the counter-proof. Corneille and Voltaire, believing themselves in this to be very knowing, do not wish us to proceed more quickly than Œdipus in the solution of his mystery. They want to have both a *coup de theâtre* upon the stage and one in the auditorium, so they leave Œdipus on one side throughout the three first Acts, and, in order to fill them, Corneille introduces Theseus and Dirce at whom the Oracle is in turn supposed to point, and Voltaire brings in the Prince Philoctetus, a former lover of Jocasta, and entertains us at some length with their liaison. Then, when they do reach the drama, they polish it off in three or four scenes. And if I were more erudite in theatrical history I am sure I could give many other such examples. . . .

The quest pursued by Œdipus is, to me, moving in the extreme. . . . I have before my eyes a man who, desperately and as though against his own desires, is seeking that which must wreak his doom. That is all I know about it ; all I want to know. Reduced to these general terms, the story of Œdipus touches me, for it might be my own. But do what I will (and it is this that disturbs and disconcerts me) I am never able to forget the precise details of this story, and the mere fact of their being present to my mind prevents me from knowing what to think or what to feel. I imagine I am listening to a drama which is above all truthful and pathetic, this drama being unfolded by the poet with the utmost gravity, " just as though it were true " ; and then suddenly a word is spoken which makes me feel that it is but a tiresome story. In short, *Œdipus Tyrannus* only moves me if I do not seek to realise the facts nor to imagine the hero's feelings after these facts have been revealed to him. Now this is a very severe condition. I am confronted with a drama the developments of which give the impression of truth, but the substance of which is improbable to the point of naïve extravagance. There is a contradiction in this, I would almost say an absurdity, which troubles me. In other words, I am interested in the drama itself in the way I should be interested in any dramatic investigation in a court of law ; but what is difficult to accept and to understand is what happened *before* and what happened *after*.

" What happened before ? " M. Francisque Sarcey will here take me up : " But that doesn't matter in the least. You must never worry a dramatic poet over his starting-point. It is a fact which he proposes to you," etc., etc. But these facts are in varying degrees difficult to assent to. The poet must not ask too much,

SOPHOCLES

and I do not believe that any drama, ancient or modern, nor any vaudeville or farce, is based upon so prodigious a postulate as *Œdipus Tyrannus.*

I don't object to the fact that no steps, or practically no steps, should have been taken to track down the murderer of Laïus, or that Jocasta and Œdipus, married for twelve years, should never have spoken of the dead King and should never have confided in each other regarding their past. That is merely improbable. But what is purely and simply impossible is what happens to Œdipus himself.

That a son, without knowing it, should have killed his father and married his own mother— this is a combination of circumstances which out of a milliard of chances will scarcely come about even once. . . . Note, moreover, that Œdipus has had foretold to him what is to happen, and that he is resolved to do everything he can to prevent it. Now, as he was so much afraid of killing his father and marrying his mother, the first precaution for him to take, one feels, was never to kill anyone except of his own age or thereabouts,* and never to marry

* Do not urge that he had been persuaded that Polybus was his father. From the moment a man of Corinth treated him as a foundling, he ought to have had his doubts.

anyone except a quite young girl, and only after having inspected her birth certificate. Acting thus, he might have had his mind at rest. But the very first thing he does after leaving Corinth is to kill an old man—and for a comparative trifle—and to wed a woman much older than himself. . . . And he has no qualms whatever ! Really, people are not quite such fools as all that !

It may be said that I am very ingenuous to discuss the verisimilitude of a tale. Well, yes, of course it is merely a tale. Some people see in it, indeed, merely a solar myth, but solar myths may be seen in all the legends and in all the narratives ever told. One has been discovered in the story of Napoleon, and I dare say we shall have one discovered presently in the *Three Musketeers* or in *Monte-Cristo* : for these solar or meteorological phenomena present to us images of life, death, resurrection, love, hate, conflict, murder, pursuit, and in these things, necessarily, we have the substance of all the stories that man has been able to extract from his brain. It seems to me fairer, however, to take the legend of Œdipus as a kind of philosophic tale for the people. The aim was to bring home this old-established truth, the melancholy axiom of accepted wisdom : " Do what you will, you cannot elude your destiny." And it was considered next what, *a priori*, would be the most terrible destiny—what would be the things that a good man would most wish not to have done ; and the answer was : to kill his father and be the husband of his mother. And thereupon the story of Œdipus came into existence, without any care being taken to ensure verisimilitude. But I feel it to be a pity that a poet, led astray by the antiquity of the legend and believing it to be well known enough to be accepted as true, should have taken it into his head to turn into a realistic drama, so to say, a tale which was in its essence symbolic. For then the tale, enacted by real living characters, will seem to me absurd, or I shall not be able to believe any longer in the drama, for a tale and a drama are two different things. And I shall be very unhappy. That is what has happened to me to-day.

I have said that what happens *afterwards* troubled me also. I allude to the feelings which Œdipus experiences when he knows all—to his bloodshot eyes and interminable lamentations. I confess all that bored me horribly ; and if everyone were sincere, everyone would say the same. Whence comes this boredom ? From the fact, surely, that it is *absolutely impossible* for me to know what I would feel if, a victim to the most fantastic of fates, I were to discover that I was the murderer of my father, the husband of my mother, the son of my wife, the brother of my children, the grandson of my father-in-law, and all that results therefrom—for it would be quite a business to trace the relationship between the son of Laïus and each of his forbears and collaterals. . . . Or rather, I very much doubt whether I should feel and act, in such circumstances, like the Œdipus of Sophocles. Let us see things as they are, or rather as they would be, and do not let us shrink from this eminently psychological problem. You discover, my good sir, that a dozen years ago, in legitimate self-defence, you unknowingly killed your father, a father whom you had never seen, and who, for his part, tried to do away with you when you were a small child. What would you feel? Nothing at all, I assure you, unless it were a great astonishment. The second discovery—that of your marriage with your mother—would, of course, trouble you more. But, after all (and if these reflections seem to you ridiculous, blame Sophocles, who forces me to indulge in them), your wife would be there, just as you have seen

her for twelve years past, you could not suppress
the past, you could not pretend that what has
been has not been, and it would not rest with
you to change the nature of the sentiments
which you have had for her and she for you, or
to regard as non-existent your second bond with
her, impious without your knowledge of the fact.
Your misfortune would be only a conception of
your mind. You would have rather the idea
that you ought to grieve than be in reality
grieved. Or rather, you would be worried not
to know what your feelings really ought to be.
It would be a case less of grief than of bewilder-
ment. If you were strong-minded, you would
go your way and leave the solution to time. If
you were weak-minded, you would kill yourself
to escape from the torment of this moral un-
certainty. Now—and this is what I find it hard
to understand—Œdipus stops short half-way : he
does not kill himself, but he tears out his eyes.

I am wrong when I say I do not understand.
What actuates Œdipus is not despair (for in this
case he would go as far as suicide), but the wish
to expiate his crime. He himself says so : he
tears out his eyes to punish himself. To punish
himself for what ? He is not guilty ; he did not
know what he was doing and *the sin is in the*

225

will, not in the material act. So much is manifest ; and now we begin to apprehend at last the thought in the mind of Sophocles. This truth, which to us appears so simple, was not much realised in those days, and that is why Sophocles wrote the drama. And knowing this truth himself, he wrote also *Antigone* and *Œdipus Coloneus*. In this latter tragedy Œdipus comes to discover that he was not at fault ; he is, indeed, on such terms with the gods that his tomb will bring happiness to the people who possess it. *Œdipus Tyrannus*, *Antigone* and *Œdipus Coloneus* form, as you know, a vast trilogy bound together less by the events than by the gradual demonstration of a moral idea. And I may admit that if, the other evening, *Œdipe Roi* had been followed by *Œdipe à Colone* the first of these tragedies would have appeared to me in quite another light.

[23 July, 1888. Vol. III.]

XVIII

COMÉDIE FRANÇAISE : *Hamlet.* Translated from
Shakespeare by Alexandre Dumas and M.
Paul Meurice.

I HAVE to talk to-day about *Hamlet* : that
is terrible ! Not only am I certain that
I shall find nothing new to say regarding
cither Shakespeare's drama or its hero, for
everything has been said already—everything,
and more than everything ; but I have forgotten
what I learnt from all those countless commentaries. I cannot even recall what I myself
said four or five months ago regarding the performance of *Hamlet* at the Porte-Saint-Martin.
My mind is all bewildered, my eyes are befogged.

What sort of person are you, Hamlet, Prince of
Denmark, you weak-willed and headstrong youth,
melancholy and violent, dreamy and brutal,
superstitious and philosophical, sensible and
mad : exquisite poet and tasteless jester : you
vivid, incoherent creature and mournful image

of the Soul in grief, individual to the point of eccentricity and generic to the point of symbolism : you, whom Shakespeare visualised as a corpulent asthmatic boy, and whom we see only as a man pale and elegant and lissom, wearing a cap and doublet of black velvet, such as befit the elder brother of Faust, such as sit well also on the earliest exponent of the modern mind, of romanticism and pessimism and nihilism and neuroticism, and many other things which doubtless never entered your mind ? We have ascribed to you so many thoughts and feelings, poor Hamlet, that you no longer resemble anything in the world, and that, in order to get back to your real features we have first to scrape away the superimposed strata of expositions and interpretations. What would I not give to see you naked with new eyes—to see you as you went forth from the hands of Shakespeare, who was assuredly one of the greatest poets of all the centuries but who, if we were frank, would still have the effect on us very often, as he had on Voltaire, of a " drunken savage."

But, after all, there is a way for me out of my misery. If I cannot see Hamlet as he really is, I can at least see him as M. Mounet-Sully has shown him to us. For, however obscure, however full of contradictions a character in a play may be, a great actor can always make him live and interpret him, by lending him a body and a soul and thus, in spite of everything, a sort of unity. Hamlet is not incomprehensible as M. Mounet-Sully has been able to play the part and as he has played it to the universal applause of the public.

In order to play Hamlet, M. Mounet-Sully has necessarily had to make a choice. Among all the Hamlets whom we have invented, he has had to pick out one and keep to him. It seems to me that the excellent tragedian has very wisely taken for an ideal on which to model himself—adapting to this ideal his mode of utterance and his whole bearing—the incomplete but comprehensible Hamlet defined by Goethe in *Wilhelm Meister*, and that he has evaded or toned down everything in the personality of the Danish Prince which remains outside this famous definition. Last spring an actor of somewhat mediocre talent gave us all that there is of hardness and fierceness in this rôle, making of Hamlet a man full of self-love and wickedness and madness. M. Mounet-Sully has been wiser. He diffuses over this same rôle an atmosphere of tenderness and melancholy. He has made Hamlet very young and very natural; he has given him a mind which is essentially gentle, pensive, languid, a mind which becomes unhinged by an appalling revelation and by the dreadful duty entailed on him by that revelation, but the violences of which are brief and as it were, involuntary. Perhaps, indeed, he has emphasised a trifle overmuch the almost feminine gentleness of the youth; in the earlier part of the play especially he has tears too continually in his voice, suggests too much the plaintive tones of a sick child or of a child suffering from great sorrow. But what an adorable Hamlet he has given us nevertheless! This unhappy boy had loved his father, had cherished a passionate devotion to him; and he sees his mother marry another man before she has worn out the shoes in which she followed the dead King to his grave. Hitherto he has been happy and full of illusions, he has believed in friendship and in the goodness of men; now, suddenly, he learns, through the voice of a ghost, that his father was killed by his uncle, with the complicity of his mother. His childlike mind cannot recover from the blow, and all his discourses and his entire conduct, strange though they may seem, may be explained by the profound

He [Hamlet]

misery into which this discovery has plunged him. At first he becomes a prey to a bitter misanthropy, ingenuous in its application to all mankind. All men become instantly in his eyes cowards and scoundrels, all women impure and unstable, the whole universe a cesspool. Hence the disproportion and the ferocity of his jesting with poor Polonius, who, if a fool, is a good old fellow. Hence the extravagance and madness (only half feigned) of his wild talk to Ophelia. He is so miserable that he would kill himself if he dared : witness the famous soliloquy. It is the custom to go into ecstasies over the deep philosophy embodied in this passage, but really its philosophy is rudimentary and banal enough. It is the utterance of a child. This " To be or not to be "—what does it all mean ? Honestly, would you understand it if what follows did not explain it ? Hamlet places among the evils which disgust him with life " the law's delays " and " the spurns that patient merit of the unworthy take."* That is an unexpected sentiment, to say the least, just here. Note that it was Voltaire who discovered this passage and gave it its vogue

* Lemaître's text here reads : " *Hamlet met parmi les maux qui le dégoutent de vivre ' les lenteurs de la procédure ' et les injustices qu'on fait aux gens de lettres.*"

in France—that should be for Shakespeare-lovers a reason for looking at it askance. . . . Forgive these irreverences, but I am expressing my thoughts freely and, as le Chassagnol says so elegantly in *Charles Demailly*, " *ceux à qui ça donne des engelures—eh bien ! J'en suis fâché !* "

Hamlet, however, cannot spend all his time soliloquising. He has to act—and what an effort it is to him to act ! He puts off acting as long as possible. First comes an orgy of scruples and precautions and preparations. He holds, to begin with, that in order to dedicate himself entirely to his task he must renounce all thoughts of love, and this is why he breaks suddenly and brutally with Ophelia. In order to gain some moments, he says to himself that perhaps the Ghost was the devil and that he has been deceived ; he would fain assure himself of his uncle's crime, and, to this end, he has represented in his presence, by a troop of actors, a crime quite similar. But, fearing that Claudius may get wind of this project and prevent it, he pretends to be mad so that no one shall suspect what he has in hand—also, because the rôle of madman suits his book in other ways, permitting him to vent his spleen and

to pose and strike attitudes. I assure you that
Hamlet poses, that he looks at himself in the
glass and likes the figure he cuts. . . . But
the moment for action does at last come, all
pretexts for procrastination have been exhausted.
The opportunity now presents itself : he finds
Claudius upon his knees, in prayer, and unconscious that someone approaches—he has
but to strike. Strike he cannot, and he finds
this admirable excuse for himself, that Claudius,
dying while he prayed, would have gone straight
to Heaven ! A little later, his mother calls
him, having remonstrances to make to him.
A curtain moves, he thinks that Claudius is
concealed behind it—he rushes upon the curtain,
and pierces it savagely with his sword. The
incident is sudden, and, like all weak men, he
is capable of such impulsive acts—above all,
when he does not see his victim. The victim
proves to be Polonius. Hamlet, beyond himself, insults and mocks the dead body. . . . Then
he turns upon his mother and, because he is
weak, because he is madder than he knows,
and because he would fain take out his own
impotence in words, he bursts into a fury,
upbraids the unhappy woman, assuming the air
of an avenging archangel, and gives way to

such excesses of rage that the Ghost appears and, taking pity on the poor trembling Queen, intervenes in the spirit of divine mercy, murmuring the words : " Speak to her, Hamlet ! Speak to her ! " Whereupon, Hamlet's heart melts. His anger over, excited nerves give way, he takes his mother in his arms, kisses her and cries like a small child.

And thus it alternates right to the end of the play : languid gloom and insensate rage. At the burial of Ophelia, he acts in a fashion that at first seems astonishing. He insults Laertes and throws himself upon him, because he, Laertes, weeps and laments too loud. Why ? Because it seems to him that Ophelia belongs to him the more in that it was through him she died : he cannot bear that any other shall presume to closer and more vocal grief for her than himself. It is perhaps remorse over her death that changes into violence, and, after all, Hamlet has been acting the rôle of madman for so long that one must ask oneself if his reason be still intact. Note that by this time we begin to have had enough of Hamlet and his feebleness and his rages and his pessimism, and his madness, whether it be assumed or real. It is about time he killed Claudius. He kills him eventually, as he was bound to kill him, without premeditation and in circumstances he has not foreseen. Altogether, there could be nothing more consistent than this character.

M. Mounet-Sully rendered with much charm and power, now the tenderness and languor of Hamlet, now the *cabotinage* with which, involuntarily, he plays the madman, now his bursts of fury, now his attempts at actions in which he loses all self-control. M. Mounet-Sully made us realise all this perfectly. The way in which he played Hamlet illumines the text of Shakespeare for us better than all the dissertations.

It is to be observed, however, that in order to maintain the unity of the part he has been obliged to soften the tone of some passages and even—so I fear—to reverse the meaning of them. When the Ghost reappears for the third or fourth time, Hamlet, who a moment ago was listening upon his knees, calls out : " Well said, old mole ! " The exclamation is surprising enough—is it terror that evokes it ? Is Hamlet already beginning to lose his head ? Or is it anxiety to maintain his coolness in front of his companions, and not to let them see he is nervous, that prompts this unseemly

jest ? I do not know. But in any case, I feel
that there can be but one way of uttering this
" old mole." It must be given out with an
unthinking roughness in which one is conscious
of a tremendous effort. Now Mounet-Sully
murmurs " old mole " in tones which would
suit the words " My adored father ! " In the
same way he recites Hamlet's distasteful
mockeries over the dead body of Polonius as
though they formed part of an elegy. He does
well, if it was only thus that he could show
us a Hamlet in some measure consistent. But,
now that I come to think about it, perhaps
that proves that the character of this Hamlet
is not so consistent as I said just now. Shakespeare's Hamlet has resort to brutalities and
ferocities of speech and conduct most of which
have been eliminated by Alexandre Dumas
and Paul Meurice, but in what is left there is
enough to disconcert us. And our doubts come
back, and those contradictions which we thought
explained, become troublesome again. This
tender and gentle youth—do what I will, I find
his conduct towards Ophelia absolutely odious.
And what wretched *cabotinage* (I must use the
word again), what puerile and extravagant
misanthropy there is in the tirades he addresses

to the poor little thing ! The revenge he takes
against the two men charged to escort him to
the King of England (a passage suppressed
in the Dumas-Meurice version) is undoubtedly
legitimate, but most certainly it is not the action
of a mind either gentle or weak or irresolute.
And then, all the contradiction in his methods
of thought ! He believes in ghosts, he believes
in the devil, in Heaven and Hell ; and he has
doubts regarding the immortality of the soul
and one may ask oneself whether he really
believes even in God !

But what does it all matter ? These contradictions, now that I note them down in
writing, cease to seem to me so serious after
all. Illogicality in one's beliefs is a profoundly
human thing and as for Hamlet's brutalities,
they are almost explicable on the ground of his
time and his race. We have to remember
that Hamlet by tradition belongs to the most
remote period of mediæval times, and by the
play to the sixteenth century as it was in
England. In short, and despite the mists which
all those commentaries and dissertations without end have accumulated round Shakespeare's
work, the figure which persists in emerging,
the image which remains unconquerably before

our eyes, is the one that Goethe saw, the one that M. Mounet-Sully made to live again the other evening. There remains, indeed, an environment of things unknown and unexplained, but this does not bother us and does but make us the more intent on the mystery in the hope of piercing it. And, indeed, thanks to this unintelligible part in his character, Hamlet resembles the more closely a live human being, for where is the man in whom there are no contradictions and who is absolutely intelligible to himself and to others? Shakespeare here, as in some of his other plays, has shown more respect for this truth than dramatic poets do usually; above all, he has simplified the human soul less than have done Corneille and Racine and Moliere. But his Hamlet is very much alive with all the mystery in the background of his nature. Besides, the impotence of will and the restlessness of thought of which the Prince of Denmark is the still ingenuous prey, are just the two diseases which have accentuated themselves most and become most widely spread during this century of ours among civilised peoples. So that even though Hamlet is a child and utters many absurdities, though his pessimism and his misanthropy are puerile and superficial, we recognise in him the germ of our own woes, we read our own malady into his and, without noticing it, introduce into his mind the minds of all the dreamers of all the men and women who have grieved and languished and known despair ever since his time, and that is why Hamlet is tremendous. Add to this the circumstance that there is no sort of spectacle which can awake in us such a wealth of memories and comparisons. The play of *Hamlet* in its subject resembles a little *The Choephori* and *Electra ;* Chateaubriand would not have failed to say that Shakespeare's hero is a Christian Orestes ; and the entire Greek drama rises up before our imagination. . . . But *Hamlet* is ancient Denmark, also Denmark in the remotest Middle Ages, half barbarous, wild and childish, a land of legends and of the supernatural, with white-bearded kings enveloped in furs. And *Hamlet* evokes simultaneously the England of the sixteenth century with its pagan Renaissance—as well as French Romanticism and Lamartine and Musset and the great stimulus given by the genius of the North to our own and the enlargement of mind which resulted for us. . . . What is there that *Hamlet* does *not* set us thinking about ? It sets as thinking of so many things that we listen to it as in a dream and cannot tell at all what the play is worth.

It does seem, however, that the first three acts are of extreme beauty. I may admit frankly that the last two, in which Hamlet is no longer to the front, seemed to me the other evening most tedious. The behaviour of Claudius is absurd. The Queen is an absolutely passive nonentity. The scene of the grave-diggers, besides being of no use at all to the play, is of a grotesque kind of drollery which has come to seem terribly banal. And so with the scene of Ophelia's madness. In the complete text it is humorous because the poor girl sings immodest things in it, but, as given at the Comédie Française, it is a scene of keepsake and romance—a chromolithograph. The flight of the years, which has benefited certain portions of Shakespeare's dramatic writings so much, has wrought great injury to others. The things that were admired most in 1830 evoke our doubts to-day.

While these two intolerable acts were unrolling themselves slowly — oh, so slowly — I grew obsessed with an idea. I asked myself what the same subject would have become in the hands of Racine. The hypothesis is not so absurd as it may appear. Supposing that Racine had lived on for a long time and not have abandoned play-writing and that, having exhausted almost everything Greek that he could imitate, he had taken, like Corneille, to turning over the old chronicles at random, he might one day have chanced on the story of Hamlet and have felt its dramatic beauty. What kind of tragedy would he have drawn forth from it? What annoys me is that I feel almost entirely incapable of replying! I believe that he would have cut out many things, either from his sense of nobility and tragic dignity or in order to observe the three unities, or on account of the scenic requirements of the theatres in his time. I believe he would have suppressed the apparition of the Ghost and have replaced it by a dream. Doubtless, he would have suppressed also the scene of the players. I do not know whether he would have retained Ophelia's madness— in any case I do not believe he would have had it represented on the stage. Would he have kept Hamlet's make-believe of madness? I think he would have suppressed this also, from his love of clarity. He might also have omitted the assault-at-arms in the last act. And then ? Well, he would certainly have developed the rôles of the Queen and Claudius and have given them more truth and life. While modifying profoundly all the external portion of the drama, and preserving the style on a plane of restrained nobility, I imagine he would have read Hamlet's character like Shakespeare, but without furnishing him with philosophical disquisitions, and that he would have kept him strictly on the confines of Goethe's future definition, without ever going outside them, perhaps without filling them out completely. Doubtless he would have brought his *Hamlet* still closer to the *Orestes* of Euripedes. His Hamlet would be neither brutal nor ferocious. He would merely intimate to Ophelia that he had no longer the right to love her, that he was dedicated entirely to a great task. Ophelia would not have fallen into the water while picking flowers but would perhaps have immolated herself with the dagger of the Princesses of Ancient Greece. Hamlet, in order to make certain as to the crime of Claudius, would find some simpler plan than the performance of the murder of Gonzago. What plan ? I cannot say. He would not treat his mother after the style of Shakespeare's hero ; he would address her with tears, listen to her confession and tell her to do penance. He would retain, however, the weaknesses, the irresolution, the terrible gloom of the English Hamlet : he would present the same " case," but it would be more clear. Claudius, I imagine, would be killed in a revolt (a revolt after the style of those in the fifth act of Quinault's tragedies) and before Hamlet should have had time to act. This *dénouement*, moreover, would be *en récit*. And this Hamlet would not give us nearly so much trouble as the Hamlet of the great " Will," but would say profound things to us, now and again, without seeming to do so, and we should be able to find romanticism and pessimism and anything we liked in him just as much as in the other . . . Only he would be easier to analyse.

[4th Oct., 1886, Vol. I.].

XIX

ODEON : *Le Songe d'une Nuit d' Eté.*   By Shakespeare.   Translated and adapted by M. Paul
Meurice.   In three Acts and eight Tableaux.

19th April, 1886.

THE resourceful Odéon, which is perhaps
at this moment the most interesting of
all the theatres of Paris, gave us last
Wednesday something which had never before
been seen in France—a fairy-play by Shakespeare
and the most fantastic of its kind : *A Midsummer
Night's Dream.*   If one of those verse-writers who
were wont formerly to make merry in lyrical
hyperboles over the solitude of the Odéon could
only have been present at this performance, he
would scarcely have known himself in face of
the poetic scenes representing the enchanted grove
and the haunts of the elves and wood-nymphs
in the moonlit bracken.   Or rather, he would
have declared : " This was bound to come, of
course.   Already some forty years ago we

detected the beginnings of vegetation in this deserted playhouse— mushrooms and even young sprouts of plants and shoots of trees were to be seen upon the stalls and actually upon the stage. Nature was resuming possession of her temple of tragedy. Since then, this vegetation has grown apace. The Odéon has developed into a virgin forest ; the moon penetrates through its creviced roof ; fairies dwell in it, elves dance in it ; and there are times when two or three young couples from the Quartier Latin, who have chanced to find out this mysterious retreat, arrange to meet here. . . . And, because of this, many people believe that *A Midsummer Night's Dream* is being played at the Odéon." Some such words might well be uttered by these jesting spirits, persisting in their jejune pleasantries. But the real truth is that the Odéon has become a living theatre and a venturesome one. They are giving things by Racine and Mélesville in it, things by Waflard and Moliére, things by Dallainval and Shakespeare. *Henriette Maréchal* and *La Fausse Agnès*, *Zaire* and *l'Arlésienne* have been played in it. They have music there, and behold ! they are now having ballets ! Actors and spectators in the Odéon are equally conscientious, ingenuous and sincere. And so eclectic a taste presides over the choice of productions that immediately after a vaudeville by Bayard we have this fairy-play of Shakespeare's, Dukes of Athens succeeding to Scribe's Colonels, Pomponne making way for Titania. M. Porel earns our gratitude by so amusing a diversity of experiment.

Moreover, he has acted handsomely by the pre-eminent poet, poet of visions and wild imaginings no less than of truth, of the delightful equally with the dreadful, him whom Ben Jonson dubbed " the Sweet Swan of Avon." He has framed this fairy-play within stage settings which charm the vision. Half close your eyes and the fairies' glade, Titania's sanctuary, the view of Athens in the final scene, are all like dreams come true. The lighting of the theatre has something fantastic and unreal about it—it is, unlike that of the sun, almost entirely from below ; it is a cold, pallid white, crude and dazzling, and yet veiled a little by the atoms of dust which float in it ; it has mystery, therefore, as well as splendour, and it is admirably adapted to a fairy-tale. Here is just the kind of shimmering, gleaming light proper to fairy-land. And in the same way the painted, rigid tree, and foliage of the scenery present, inevitably, the unnatural aspect that befits a magic woodland ; they lack grace and there is no trembling, no whispering of leaves. There is no mystery in the demi-obscurity of dense copses through which breezes blow and in which may be heard the murmuring of swarms of living things : mystery is to be found only in absolute silence, in an effulgence with the branches of the trees all glistening. The mystery is in the light itself. Of course it was not thus that Shakespeare imagined his enchanted forest. But, mystery for mystery, this forest delights. It is almost the " extra-natural " and purely metallic scenery dreamt of by Baudelaire. And to complete the spell, this feast for the eyes is enveloped in music—the soul of the forest finding expression in Mendelssohn's melodies. (It is exquisite music, but, to tell the truth, it did not seem to me fanciful enough, not moon-lit enough, save only the Nocturne in the third Act. The soul of the forest—so I felt—should not sing quite so smoothly and correctly : I could almost say that it has been too. well taught. I am about to utter a blasphemy, but I was set thinking of certain other melodies which issued from the brain of that strange, faun-like being, Maurice Rollinat, disturbing melodies which seem to flow down your spinal column like a caress. . . .) And, in addition to the orchestra of M. Colonne, we are given choruses and soloists and a troop of ballet-dancers into the bargain. Dancing at the Odéon! Imagine it! And, as though wishful to see us die of happiness, M. Porel has been prodigal of precious materials and has sent cascades of gold and jewels down the silk surfaces of the costumes. The State ought certainly to convey its compliments to M. Porel—and then perhaps to place him under control of a Trustee, by reason of his Neronian extravagance.

And now let us look at Shakespeare's Dream. We are present at the wedding of Theseus, Duke of Athens, with Hippolyte, Queen of the Amazons. It is taking place in a palace built in Renaissance style. The Duke wishes to bring about another marriage—that of Prince Demetrius and Princess Hermia. But Hermia does not love Demetrius — she loves and is loved by Prince Lysander. And Demetrius is loved by Princess Helena, whom he does not love. It is the song from *Carmen* once again :

" Si tu ne m'aimes pas, je t'aime—"

Lysander plans with Hermia that he shall carry her off, and they arrange a meeting in the forest. Helena attaches herself lovingly but despairingly to Demetrius, answering all his rough words to her with " I love you ! " All these lovers have a strange and delicious way of talking love ; they combine in their utterances the rhetoric of the Renaissance, the ingenuity of the Euphuists, and the simplicity of a passion which is true and deep. And what a delight it is to hear the words from the lips of characters hailing from Greece, the mythical Greece of pre-Homeric times, and who have such names as Helena, Demetrius, Theseus, Hippolytus ! Those three words alone, " Theseus, Duke of Athens," open wide the gates of dreamland. Did Shakespeare really intend that ? Or is it sheer simplicity in him ? In any case, there is suddenly conjured up in our minds a delectable blend of memories and impressions, and I believe we feel an enjoyment keener than Shakespeare's own because Greece means more to us than it did to him and his contemporaries. . . . Theseus in a doublet, Theseus expressing himself like the wits of the Court of Queen Elizabeth, Theseus dwelling in a palace which must have been built by some sixteenth century Italian, and which adjoins a northern forest without olive or oleander, but inhabited by elves and fairies—what a pleasant dream ! We enjoy at once two kinds of poetry,

two kinds of mythology, two kinds of humanity.
What a savourless thing mere " local colour " is,
compared with these inventions! There is no
poetry to touch this masquerade of the ages
which places in the thoughts of one century the
habits of another. After all, it is only in this
fashion that a poet can create true human beings
not foreseen by God. And according as the
centuries roll past, these associations become
richer and richer. Shakespeare was able to mix
the soul of his time only with very few traditions
of ancient Greece, whereas we who now listen
to his work are enabled by the greater distance
we have travelled from it, and by the knowledge
that has since accumulated, to find strange
charms in it of which Shakespeare had no
suspicion, so that we may say that we add our
own soul to his. And thus do we enrich Shakespeare, and he in some measure becomes our
creation.

And we do the same for all the poets of the
past. There are many things in the poetry of
former times which we love, not merely for their
inherent grace or piquancy or beauty, but also
because they are so far away from us and so
characteristic of an age different from our own :
we love them, therefore, twice as much as they

were loved by contemporaries. In Theodore de Banville's *Beau Léandre* the tale of the carrying off of Octave by the Barbary pirates recalls to us in a single flash Plautus and Terence, the Italian comedy, the *Fourberies de Scapin* and half the *dénouements* of Moliére. And this one line—

" *Messine est une ville étrange et surannée—*"

gives us perhaps more pleasure than our ancestors got out of all the stories of pirates told in all the comedies, for they found theirs merely in a narrative coloured with romance. Whereas, think first of all that is contained in Banville's thirty lines—their irony, the poetry of the remote, and, in an archaic conceit, a form and method of versification which one feels to be of to-day. I firmly believe that our æsthetic joys are subtler and deeper than those of the men of past ages. I am always tempted to say with Philaminte to the poets of old :

" *Mais quand vous écriviez ce charmant 'Quoi qu' on die,'*
En avez-vous senti, vous, toute l'énergie ? "

The last man at this rate will die from feeling beauty to excess. And, if I am not mistaken, that is really the idea which Stéphane Mallarmé

sought to express in a kind of fairy-tale, the end
of which has been revealed to me by one of his
friends. The scene takes place during the last
days of the world. The few men who still survive,
richly apparelled like the favourites of Henri III,
move forward cautiously ; for the crust of the
globe, consumed by internal fires, has now the
thickness only of a sheet of paper. A star
appears on the horizon. The last men look at it
ecstatically and exclaim in unison : " Beautiful ! "
That is all. It is their last utterance, for the
shock communicated to their bodies by the vision
of beauty has reacted on the terrestrial surface
and the abyss has engulfed them. . . .

But let us return to our *Midsummer Night's
Dream*. From the palace of Theseus, Shakespeare transports us to the workshop of Quince
the Carpenter. We are now in the midst of an
actual world of living men. A company of good
friends and comrades, Bottom the Weaver, Flute
the Bellows-mender, Snout the Tinker, and others
are preparing a dramatic performance in celebra-
tion of the marriage of the noble Duke. They
will play *Pyramus and Thisbe*. Quince the Carpenter is giving out the parts. Bottom will be
Pyramus, Flute the Bellows-mender will be
Thisbe. Another will be Lion, before whom

Thisbe will flee. Another will be Moonlight and will hold up a lantern, because it is by moonlight that the two lovers have to meet. Another will be Wall, and through the holes in Wall they will tell their love : for this, he will whiten himself with plaster, his spread-out fingers representing the holes in the wall. There are jests of a somewhat fantastic and ponderous description, written for the Anglo-Saxons of three hundred years ago (as it would seem) and recalling, to ever so slight an extent, the witticisms of M. Meilhac in the *Demoiselles Clochart*. But Bottom is a caricature of a broad and genuine kind. This rustic is full of the frank and diverting vanity of the professional actor ; he wants to play Thisbe, he wants to play Lion, he wants to play Wall, he wants to play all the parts, and he insists on verses fifteen feet long. They are amusing creatures, the whole lot of them ; some of them full of beer and well-filled out, the others thin and pale and wretched-looking. . . . No doubt the poet shows us these good folk in order to throw into relief the fantastic world which he is about to conjure up. Bottom and Quince will make Puck and Titania more ethereal still.

A flash of wings and we are in the Fairies' Glade ! This woodland of the North is as

different from the sacred grove wherein Œdipus
finds a resting-place as the soul of Shakespeare
is from the soul of Sophocles. Instead of laurels
and green oaks etching against the blue heavens
their dark and gleaming foliage, Shakespeare's
forest (which the Odéon's scenes, though so
beautiful, certainly misrepresent) is one of huge
trees that sway and tremble, of towering sylvan
colonnades whose feet are sunk in the surge of
bracken, of moonbeams stealing down into the
undergrowth, and of endless stirrings and rustlings
and whisperings and flittings of beings invisible
—instinct with the sense of a hidden, secret,
teeming life. Instead of nymphs whose clear-
cut outlines are but graceful symbols, nymphs
whom our poets of old invented but never
visualised, here we have fairies and elves, little
people with wings, children of the moon who
might well be denizens of these dark glades,
palpitating with life and whom one almost
imagines one has seen for oneself. . . . Instead
of smiling fancies, limited in their scope, and
leaving no disquiet in the heart, here is the
Dream, offspring of the lands of mist and solitude,
the feeling of the mystery which, beneath outward
forms, pervades all existence. Instead of the
tranquil and unspeculative devotion to mother-

earth, the harvest-giver, here is a passion for
nature, a loving quest for her beauties, a vague
and inexpressible yearning to communicate—
how, one knows not—with the limitless soul
encompassing us. . . . Note, please, that in this
Midsummer Night's Dream there is a new
sentiment, of which a foretaste doubtless may
be found in Spenser's *Faery Queen* and which
perhaps was latent in the Celtic legends, but
which assuredly does not come from the Latins
or the Greeks—a sentiment which our Renaissance
never knew, of which our seventeenth century
had no inkling and which began to blossom with
us—to our shame, be it said—only with Jean-
Jacques Rousseau, and very modestly even then.

Now, in this forest live Oberon and Titania
and Puck—Puck the Divine, that Wit of Dreamland, a diminutive figure of fantasy who philo-
sophises astride a moonbeam.   Puck is jeweller
to the flowers : he supplies the Carnation with
a ruby, the Easter Daisy with gold, hangs pearls
in the Cowslips' casket ; and the flowers pay him
with kisses. But Puck is also a sage. This elf
of the forest has all the wisdom which is acquired
by forest-dwellers : he knows the vanity of
human passions, but he knows too that if they
deceive, if they bring suffering, there is the source

of life in them as well; and his knowledge expresses itself in a kindly mockery. He is full, moreover, of such wild and joyous imaginings as are only right in a person so small, so pretty, and so shrewd; and from afar one might take the trills of his laughter for the notes of a nightingale.

Puck knows the story of Hermia and Lysander, and of Demetrius and his love for Hermia, and of Helena who is loved by nobody. And to amuse himself a while, he distils upon the eyes of Demetrius and Lysander the juice of a magic flower whose virtue is such that on awakening they will both love the person who shall first be seen by them. This person is Helena; and both in turn address words of passion to the young girl who hitherto has been disdained and who takes their declarations for a cruel sport. . . . A very subtle mockery of love, charming and saddening. For, I ask you, what makes us love? Helena is not less beautiful than Hermia, and she has the more tender way with her. Why do Lysander and Demetrius love Hermia and not Helena? They themselves do not know. And why, now, do they love Helena and not Hermia? Again, they do not know. Merely because the essence of a flower has been sprinkled upon their eyelids while they slept, for a reason

257

R

they are ignorant of, as in the former case—
from an impulse irrational and inexplicable :

> " Il existe un bleu dont je meurs
> Parce qu'il est dans des prunelles."

But if this same shade and depth of blue—
absolutely the same—were to be found in another
pair of eyes, perhaps they would not win my
love ! Why not ?

Not only can love never tell exactly what
determines its choice, but this choice is often
unworthy and dishonouring, without love's knowledge. Love, capricious and inexplicable ever,
is often ridiculous and blind. Often the heart
goes to a blue in the eyes that is not there.
And this is the second truth which our wicked
Puck will demonstrate. Oberon is angry with
Titania because he suspects the Queen of the
Fairies of cherishing a tender sentiment for a
youth, the son of the King of the Indies. Puck,
to minister to his master's feeling of resentment,
touches Titania's eyelids with his magic flower
while she sleeps ; then when the company of
Smug the Joiner come into the forest to rehearse
their play, he leads Bottom aside and puts on
him an ass's head. And it is Bottom whom
Titania first sees on awakening. What angel,

she exclaims, has waked her from her flowery bed ! And when he brays in answer she declares she is enamoured of his voice. Upon which Bottom brays again and asks for oats. Presently the little fairy rests her satiny pink cheek against the ass's rough and unresponsive muzzle. Her bud-like mouth kisses the dark moist snout and her tiny hands caress the long stiff ears. And Titania summons the wood-nymphs, who come and girdle the ass's head with roses, and circle round him in a rhythmic dance. . . . The contrast is so strong, the symbolism so expressive and so clear, the scene so fantastic and so daring in its charm, that it is sweet and melancholy and comical all at once—you are saddened and delighted and amazed !

[19th April, 1896. Vol. I.]

XX

THEATRE CHOISI D'IBSEN : *Les Revenants* . . .
Translation by M Prozor. Preface by M.
Edouard Rod.

SOMETIMES I feel wretched and ashamed
of myself for knowing only my native
language, a little Latin and a very little
Greek ; and I ask myself how it can be possible
that I followed our Lower Course in German for
eight years and the Middle Course for one year
(for a change) without learning a single word of
the language of Goethe and of Hegel. And I
tell myself that, knowing only one literature, I
know nothing ; that extremely interesting ways
of understanding and expressing life escape me
altogether, and that the world is much less
varied and much less amusing for me than it is
for those who understand foreign tongues and
who have visited other countries. I reflect that
one has no right really to be, to such a degree
as I am, a Man of the Centre, no better than a
vine-dresser of Touraine ; that one ought not

to drowse away in a condition of such incuriosity or in so jealous a devotion to the hereditary soil.

Fortunately, there are translations. For some years past they have been abundant enough to furnish even a poor monoglot like me with some idea of the different European literatures. I know, of course, that a part, and sometimes the best part, of the talent of the writers disappears necessarily in the translation, however accurate and efficient this may be. I wonder what can survive of Racine or La Fontaine, translated into English or German ! Probably the loss involved is not less than for some of the authors who are translated into French. But what they lose in one respect, it seems to me these authors may gain in another, and I shall endeavour to tell you why.

In the writers of my own country, even in some of the best of them, I become conscious of a certain form of phraseology, some species of rhetorical device acquired or invented, systematic literary artifices ; and in the long run all this begins to irritate me. Now, the same must, one feels sure, be the case with foreign writers also. But just these idiosyncrasies are not transposable into another tongue, they are not shown us in the translation. Or, rather, their rhetorical method, if they have one, seems to us original and delectable. In passages which are, perhaps, mediocre or bad they appear to us merely bizarre, and perhaps these are the passages which I feel most inclined to enjoy, in order not to look like a man entirely devoid of all feeling for the exotic.

On the other hand, when these authors are excellent and when they move me, they move me through and through. For then I can be sure that it is only by the force of their thought, the truth of their pictures, or the sincerity of their emotions, that they have acted on me. It is clear that at these moments the substance in them is not to be distinguished from the form ; I feel, even in the translations, that all the words are necessary, and other words could not be used. The local accent has suddenly vanished ; and, encountering in the work of these " barbarians " things that are beautiful in exactly the same way as the beautiful things of our own writers, I experience a pleasure which is doubled by surprise and which is pleasantly tinged with gratitude.

And thus, whether in the moments when their rhetorical devices and their possible banality escape me, or in those moments when they dispense with rhetorical devices altogether, I am continually getting the impression of something frank and ingenuous and genuine and spontaneous and profoundly interesting, even in those parts of their work in which they are clumsy or tedious or obscure. In this neutral garb, this kind of ill-cut costume which is a translation, beneath these French words disguising a writer who is not French, old truths and familiar reflections produce upon me the effect of strange novelties. I seek and discover in them a savour, a colour, a perfume. I tell myself that these foreigners combine with the refinements of feeling and thought of late-comers into the world of letters the candour and sincerity which we associate with the primitives. And I become quite excited over them, and I also come near to saying (as do to-day so many people of high authority) : " What are our writers of romance compared with Tolstoi and George Eliot ? What are our poets compared with Shelley and Rossetti ? And, finally, although our dramatic authors may be, without doubt, better workers, how far removed they are from the deep humanity and calm daring of an Ibsen, an Ostrowsky or a Pisemsky ! "

Then I shut up their books ; I calm myself ;

IBSEN

I muster my memories and begin to institute comparisons. These works which have struck me, now and again, by their incontestable beauty and, more still, by their strangeness of accent, the substance of them, I perceive, is not so new as it seemed just at first, for the same substance is to be found in books of our own which, ingrates that we are, we have almost forgotten. And at this point I do not, indeed, cease to esteem and even to admire these foreigners, or to thank them for the little thrill of pleasure or enthusiasm they have given me, but I have no longer any illusions about them. I see that the things which I admired in them with most sincerity are the things in which they most resemble ourselves. . . . I have travelled enough. I close my door behind me, I become a Latin and a Gaul again and resume the predilections and prejudices of the narrow-minded peasant and aboriginal that I am.

Such has been the sequence of feelings that I have passed through during the last week or so while reading translations of certain Norwegian, Russian and English plays, of which I propose to discourse to you during my month's vacation.

265

THEATRICAL IMPRESSIONS

I begin with Henrik Ibsen, whose best known dramas, *Ghosts* and *The Doll's House*, M. Prozor has translated. I find some details about Ibsen in the remarkable Preface by M. Edouard Rod and in the translator's notes. Ibsen is now a man of sixty. He had a hard youth. His first writings were some verses addressed to the Hungarians to encourage them in their struggle (1848), a series of sonnets to King Oscar of Sweden, urging him to support the interests of their Danish brothers, and a play about Catiline, in which this conspirator is presented as an Utopian, a dreamer, a humanitarian. Then comes a period of tranquillity ; Ibsen now writes some quite ordinary pieces, and becomes Director of the Christiania Theatre. But the spirit of revolt reappears in *Love's Comedy*, *The Pillars of Society*, *Ghosts*, *The Doll's House*, *Rosmersholm*, and, above all, in *Emperor and Galilean*.

It is in the name of a thoroughgoing and uncompromising Christianity that Ibsen takes his stand against the conventions and hypocrisies. But at the same time (so we are told) this mournful man, this thinker of the Far North, professes to regret the naturalistic conception of human life held in ancient times. As M. Edouard Rod explains, " Ibsen understands the historical need for the coming of Christianity without admiring it or loving it without ceasing to appeal to a ' Third Kingdom,' which he does not define but which is to embody a reconciliation between the theory of the right to enjoy life, which is the foundation of Pagan beliefs, and that of renunciation, which is the basis of the new doctrines."

The volume is embellished with a portrait of Ibsen : rough-hewn features, piercing eyes, mouth shut tight, a thick, untidy shock of hair, the aspect of an old Scandinavian sailor. He lived for a long time in Rome, then in Munich, in complete solitude. Such is Ibsen, the Puritan.

But, on the other hand, our Polar Bear has managed a theatre, an avocation which is apt to lack austerity. M. Prozor tells us, moreover, that this revolutionary has a son in the diplomatic service, that he likes to adorn his frock-coat with a string of Orders when he goes out into Society, that he is not insensible to feminine flattery, and that in Stockholm and Christiania he has his little battalion of fair admirers. Here we have the partisan of the *joie de vivre*. . . . Good !

Ghosts is an energetic, almost ferocious, defence

of the *joie de vivre* as against religious gloom, of nature as against law, of individualism as against the oppression exercised by social prejudices. I will not say that the thought in it is always as clear as the feeling. But in spite of intolerable *lenteurs* and sometimes of passages which are somewhat obscure, the drama grips you and holds you until the end. It is true and deep. A soul's revolution, one of most intense and most universal interest, is set forth in it with power and audacity, and with a sort of wild *élan*. This is the moral crisis of the virtuous, meditative and proud-minded Hélène Alving.

Fru Alving is the widow of a captain who had been a Chamberlain to the King. The first year of her marriage was a hard one : her husband was a horrible debauchee. Once she went so far as to flee from home and seek refuge in the house of a clergyman, Pastor Manders, for whom she felt a certain *tendresse*. But the pastor, who is a good man, recalled her to a sense of duty and led her back to her husband. From this moment it became a matter of public notoriety that Captain Alving had turned over a new leaf. He had given proof of this by works of charity, he had died full of all the virtues,

and his wife felt the wish to consecrate his
memory by erecting a House of Refuge which
should bear the name of the deceased.

Fru Alving has a son, Oswald, whom she sent
to Paris when he was quite young, and who has
become a painter of talent. Oswald has just
come home to his mother's to take some months'
rest. While Manders and Fru Alving are dis-
cussing this pious Foundation, Oswald interrupts
them and scandalises the worthy Pastor by the
cool cynicism of his remarks and, above all, by
his defence of the free and easy *ménages* of Paris.
When the young man goes out :

" What do you say to that, Fru Alving ? "
asks the Pastor.

And Fru Alving replies : " I say that Oswald
is perfectly right ! "

And soon we learn the truth : Fru Alving confesses it with a sombre pride. The truth, to begin
with, is that for the last eighteen years she has
played a courageous comedy, hiding from all
eyes the continued drunkenness and debauchery
of her husband, right down to his death ! . . . " I
had to put up with many things in that house,"
she says : " To keep him at home in the evenings
and at night, I had to be the companion of his
secret orgies ; up above, in his room, I had to

sit at table with him, *tête-à-tête*, clinking glasses with him and drinking and listening to his mad harangues. I have had to wrestle with him to get him to bed." The truth, further, is that Fru Alving, as the outcome of her reflections, has become completely disenchanted with virtue. While she was doing heroic things she had gradually sloughed off all her prejudices and beliefs. But she does not regret her painful sacrifices, since they were for her son. She sent him away so that he should know nothing of his father's ignominy. . . . Ah, if only the son shall not have inherited the father's vices ! . . . Fru Alving has just told the Pastor that once she surprised her husband alone with the house-maid. "Leave me alone, leave me alone, Kammerherr ! "* the girl was crying out ! . . . While Fru Alving is still telling of this incident the sound of a chair being knocked over is heard from the dining-room, followed by the words :

"Oswald, are you mad ? Let me go ! " It is Regina, the daughter of that former servant, attacked in her turn by the Kammerherr's son !

There they are, the "Ghosts" ! . . In the

* Captain Alving was a Chamberlain to the King. The title *Kammerherr* is used thus, like Admiral or Captain.

Act which follows, Fru Alving says to the Pastor : " When I heard Regina and Oswald in the next room it was as if the past had come back before my eyes. I am almost inclined to believe, Pastor, that we are all of us ghosts."

But the " Ghosts " are not merely the parents and the ancestors re-born in their children. They are something else as well (and this double interpretation of the same word, it must be admitted, scarcely contributes to the clearness of the work) : they are, also, in each one of us, the ideas and prejudices we have imbibed and which act on us all without our knowledge. " It is not only the blood of our fathers and mothers that flows in our veins, there is also within us a kind of wrecked idea, a sort of dead belief and all that results therefrom. It is not living, but it is none the less there, at the bottom of ourselves, and we shall never succeed in freeing ourselves from it. . . . It seems to me that the land is peopled by ghosts, that there are as many of them as there are grains of sand on the sea-shore. And then—all of us, whatever our numbers—we are so wretchedly in fear of the light ! "

The rest of the play shows us Fru Alving doing all she can to lull to sleep, by satiating it, the impure and deplorable " Ghost " which is in Oswald, and to this end driving out of herself with the fury of revolt those other " Ghosts "— the doctrines and prejudices of her Christian and Puritan upbringing. She recognises now, she declares, that she was misguided in doing what she had believed to be her duty. She startles Pastor Manders by reproaching him for having rejected her formerly when she came to him to throw herself into his arms. " Why," exclaimed the saintly man, " that was the greatest victory of my whole life—a triumph over myself ! " " Say, rather, a crime against us both ! " " What ! when I begged and implored of you—when I said to you : ' Woman, return to him who is your husband before the law ! '—when you, almost out of your mind, came crying to me, ' Here I am, take me ! ' You call that a crime ! " " Yes, so it seems to me." And, in truth, but for this stupid sacrifice she would not have brought into the world an unfortunate child, incurably tainted, body and soul ; and thus it has come about that the mother's virtue is to blame in a way for the physical and moral misfortunes of the son.

For Oswald confesses to her, in a scene of strange beauty, that he is doomed, altogether doomed. He can no longer work; he is suffering from dreadful nervous troubles and from a softening of the spinal cord and other things. A Paris doctor whom he has consulted has said to him : " There has been some kind of rottenness going on in you ever since your birth." And the old cynic added : " The sins of the fathers fall on the children."

That is why Oswald asks unceasingly for brandy or for champagne ; and that is why, the moment he set eyes on Regina, he threw his arms round her. " Mother ! " he exclaimed afterwards, " when I saw that splendid-looking girl in front of me, so pretty and so full of health . . . I had a revelation that in her was my chance of getting well. It was the *joie de vivre* I saw in front of me. Oh, mother, that *joie de vivre !*—in this country you hardly know what it is. . . . The *joie de vivre* and then the joy of working ! Oh, it's really, at bottom, the same thing. But this joy also is unknown to you people here. Here one is taught to regard work as the scourge of God, a punishment for one's sins, and to think of life as a miserable thing from which we can never be delivered soon enough."

Fru Alving : A vale of tears, yes. And,

S

truly, we apply ourselves conscientiously to
making it one.

Oswald : " But in Paris they won't hear of
such a notion ! There one can feel full of joy
and happiness merely because one is alive.
Mother, have you noticed that everything I have
painted has had to do with the joy of living ?
The joy of living everywhere and all the time ! "
. . . He wants his mother to sit by his side and
drink with him ; she obeys. He wants her to
call in Regina so that Regina may drink with
them also ; the mother consents. " Now I understand everything," Fru Alving murmurs. " It
is the first time I have realised the whole truth.
My son, you shall know everything exactly, and
then you can come to a decision."

What is it that she has to tell him ? The
scene, interrupted at this point by an ironical
incident—the burning down of the charitable
institution which had been erected to the memory
of Captain Alving and which Pastor Manders had
refused to insure lest he should seem to harbour
doubts of Providence. It is resumed in the
following Act. While Oswald was speaking of
the joy of living, his mother had suddenly understood that it was the undue suppression of this
joy in the little northern town and in his dismal

274

home that had been the ruin of Alving and had thrown him into his disordered manner of life. " I myself," she proceeds to say, " had a bringing up in which there was question only of duties and obligations, and for long that was the basis of my own existence, which consisted only of duties—my duties, *his* duties, etc., etc. I fear I made our home insupportable to your poor father, Oswald ! " Henceforth she will be able to pardon the dead man and to speak out freely to his son who will understand and forgive. Fru Alving also reveals to Regina that she is Oswald's half-sister.

What, then, are Fru Alving's hopes ? Here, as in several other parts of the play, one would like to have a little more clarity. Has she counted on this revelation sufficing to calm Oswald and helping him to live henceforth tranquilly—ill-regulated youth that he is—in proximity to the good-looking wench ? Or, in the event of the young neuropath wanting to go beyond all bounds, is it possible that she would acquiesce ? * Certain passages seem to justify our assuming so. One cannot tell how far a woman of the North may go when she breaks away from Puritanism !

* On re-reading the play later Lemaître discovered that Fru Alving's disposition to acquiesce is made clear in Act II.

Happily, from the moment she learns that she
cannot marry him, Regina (who represents the
joie de vivre in its simplest, most natural, and
most animal form) has no inclination to be the
young master's hospital nurse. " And so my
mother was . . ." she murmurs and goes off
light-heartedly, determined to follow suit !

The invalid becomes more and more miserable.
" Oswald, has this disturbed you greatly ? " his
mother asks him. " You mean all this business
about father ? " " Yes, about your father. I'm
afraid the effects of what I've told you have been
too much for you." " What makes you think
that ? Naturally, I have been extremely surprised, but really it is all the same to me." " All
the same to you that your father was so profoundly unhappy ? " " Oh, I can feel pity for
him as for anybody else, but——" " Nothing
more ? For your poor father ? " " My father ?
My father ? I have no recollection of him, except
once that he made me sick by making me smoke."
" It is terrible when one thinks of it ! Ought not
a child to have some love for his father, in spite
of everything ? " " When the father has no
claim on his gratitude ? When the child has
never known him ? And you, mother, so
enlightened about everything else, do you really

cling to this old prejudice ? " " Is it really
nothing but a prejudice ? " " Oh, well, it is one
of the prevalent ideas which the world accepts,
without reflection and——" Fru Alving to
herself, much moved : " Ghosts ! "

More " ghosts " for her to rid her own mind
of ! She had been feeling that it was " only
right " that the son should not curse the father,
and this was the reason why she had spoken.
And this last involuntary return to the habits of
mind, the moral conventions which had been the
cause of her life's misery, has the result only of
hastening on the crisis to which her child must
succumb ! The sick man feels that this crisis is
now impending, and he knows that if it does
not kill him it will leave him in a condition of
complete imbecility :

" Oh, the pain of it ! . . . I had a return of
it down there. It went quickly, but I have been
followed, tortured, persecuted by the pain, and
I came hurrying back to you as quickly as I
could. Ah, if it were a question of only some
ordinary fatal disease ! . . . But there's something so horrible about this ! The notion of
returning to the condition of a small child—to
require to be fed, to be . . . oh, there are no
words to express how I suffer. . . . And you

have taken Regina from me ! Why isn't she here ? *She* would have come to my help ! " He explains to his mother that should the attack return he has in his pocket a little box of morphia powder and that she must give it to him. Fru Alving feels she could not. . . . " Ah ! " exclaims Oswald, " Regina would not have hesitated long over it ; Regina had such an adorably light heart." The crisis comes—a dreadful scene, this. The sun now bursts forth in full splendour— hitherto the action has taken place in con- tinuously gloomy weather, with the rain falling ; the sick man, motionless, his eyes glazed, to all seeming a corpse, says in a heavy, toneless voice : " Mother, give me the sun, the sun, the sun ! " He does not stir and can say no more. . . . The mother, heart-broken, looks in Oswald's pocket for the box of morphia. . . . Is she going to make use of it herself ? . . . The curtain falls.

*   *   *

Last Monday I was able only to describe the action of Ibsen's " Ghosts," and, even so, had to restrict myself to the main action. It remains for me to tell you the impressions left on my mind by this play and what I was able to make of it.

IBSEN

The work is outwardly peaceful, slow in movement, and as though wrapped in snow. The background is the coast of one of the great fjords of Northern Norway ; the setting is singularly peaceful : a great scantily-furnished drawing-room, with, at the back, a conservatory, through the windows of which may be seen the melancholy fjord across a veil of rain. The scenes follow each other in a drab atmosphere, the interminable dialogues reminding one of the rain which beats unceasingly against the window-pane. In this setting we have one of the most violent dramas a man can conceive—a drama of the mind, of the conscience, in its silent way appalling, with some sudden outbursts. . . .

M. Édouard Rod, in his Preface, gives us a pretty picture of the social habits and manners of these distant regions of Norway. " We see a life extremely regular and peaceful, the life of a small, happy country which has no history, little towns in which everyone knows everyone else, and in which the surface of the sleeping waters is occasionally troubled only by old wives' gossiping. . . ." A sky which prescribes meditation and self-communing ; a social circle gathered around a porcelain stove ; a pleasant leisureliness of thought and feeling ; a sense of security,

rooted in accepted traditions ; a great gravity
and a great calm. . . . Very little opening for
external pleasures or amusements. Yes, but
plenty of time for reflection ! And, doubtless,
reflection for most of these tranquil creatures
amounts only to drowsy dreamings in front of
glasses of beer and in the smoke ascending from
pipes or in the eternal re-reading of the well-
thumbed Bible : in short, to mere ruminations.
(For the " free examination," the basis of
Protestantism, seems to me, when thought of
in connection with the flock of the faithful, a
mere pleasantry ; and to contrast Protestant
freedom of mind with Catholic docility is to trifle
with us.) For the exceptional few, however, this
reflection results in the development of the
individual life. Now, individual life almost
always means revolt against the rules of collective
life. It is therefore to be believed that beneath
this apparent tranquillity, beneath this material
discipline, of the Northern peoples there lie
hidden in more than one mind strange audacities
of thought. They remain quite theoretical and
unexpressed, and they accommodate themselves
to the traditional yoke. But when they do
break out ! . . .

It would appear that at this moment we

IBSEN

French are perceptibly ahead of the other races of Europe. At all events we are not, we and other races, at the same point of political development ; and, as it can scarcely be maintained that we are behind them, it follows that we must be in front. We have reached, it is true, an unlucky moment, a time of transition when something, we don't know what, is being prepared and elaborated. But the advance which a race may have made along the road of progress is not necessarily to be measured by its prosperity. It is a thing worthy of note that we have a national anthem which could not be sung before rulers of the other European nations if they happened to come to see us. And yet we have no wish to disown the *Marseillaise*. Our case, then, is a unique one. If it does not do to boast about it, we must not blush for it. This means that something has been achieved by us which still remains to be achieved elsewhere. For a century past we have been making experiments for the benefit of others. But (apart from our first efforts of a century since) I venture to say that we are making these experiments gently and that we do not push them to extremes ; it seems as though we were not very certain of the excellence of our aims. We have among us few serious revolutionaries. They are either mere blunderheads or else mere men of business ; or else they are amateurs and are too elegant and too clever, There is a touch of the Latin *gouailleur*, sometimes, about even the most determined and most dangerous of our anarchists. . . .

When the races of the North, with their Puritan habits of mind, shall begin in their turn to make experiments, be sure that it will be a quite different affair. They will very soon catch us up. They will turn the world upside down conscientiously, scrupulously, systematically and with a thoroughness worthy of imbibers of beer. It is to them that we owe the greatest religious revolution of modern times. Perhaps it is to them we shall be indebted presently for the supreme transformation of human existence in the West.

All this by way of explaining that Fru Alving is an entirely serious rebel. For twenty years she led her life in conformity with the Christian ideal of duty and in exceptionally painful circumstances. Not only did she sacrifice her youth and her heart, but she has had to add to this effort towards absolute renunciation a still greater effort at keeping up an heroic lie which was to have the effect of disguising her renunciation.

IBSEN

A woman of the Latin race would have found some way of bringing some graciousness to this task, and perhaps even some touch of insouciance and gentleness. Fru Alving has been able to achieve her painful duty only at the cost of an unceasing tension of her whole being. She has achieved it all too seriously, she has given too much thought to it. And it is through having thought too much that she has grown to have doubts. She has reflected too much on life. Now, believers of the type of Fru Alving are incapable of drawing short at a provisional solution. If the falsity of their conception of life is suddenly revealed to them, they conclude it is the contrary conception that is true. They go straight from the affirmation to the negation. What is noted by the votary of a dogmatic religion during the hours when he imagines he can detach himself from it is the absence of all rule and all belief. That is why, nine times out of ten, unfrocked priests fall into the most complete moral anarchy.

And if, in spite of all, the world had no meaning? How absurd to have sacrificed to a nothing the twenty best years of her life, irrecoverable years! Once started, Fru Alving will never stop. For her, the choice is between immolation of her whole being to the rule of Christ and a full and free enjoyment of existence : between the Christian ideal and the Pagan ideal. Her profound nature cannot conceive of any intermediate course. A French woman would embrace the new ideal without talking about it, perhaps without the knowledge that she was doing so, and while retaining something of the old. We thrive on these minglings and inconsistencies. But Fru Alving can change only through and through, consciously and violently.

And yet in the first part of the play Mme. Alving is still hesitant. It would seem that she has never completely lost her faith, and that her misfortunes and her experience of life have but added to it a kind of detached philosophy, indulgent and ironical. It is the final blow which destroys her old beliefs and, so to speak, uproots her soul. This final blow is one of those cruel and horrible absurdities which, when we encounter them in our own lives, make us feel desperate. Her son, the child for whom she has borne so much (it was to prevent him from suspecting the shame of his father that she parted herself from him and kept up her tragic comedy)—her son is struck down unjustly, brutally, in a way that baffles understanding. Because the father had been a poor wretch who, being bored by his dull surroundings, took to drink and to philandering, the son must be a weakling with a diseased spine, and die an idiot at twenty. And there would have been nothing of all this had she but taken her supposed duty less seriously—had she not felt obliged to return home after her flight to the Pastor's house. It is now that Fru Alving breaks out. She has been a dupe too long and life is too stupid. Good-bye to faith and to rules of conduct and to regard for what is " right " and what is " proper " ! And just as this child of hers, now soon to die, can think of nothing but enjoyment of the life which is being taken from him, so she in her turn is the victim of a feeling of revolt against useless suffering. It is like a new Gospel which has come to her, all too late. But if she can no longer profit by it herself, at least she will do what she can to prevent her stricken son from being denied the joys—what matter if they be gross joys ?—this miserable world has to offer. Let him drink, then, if he can get any pleasure out of it and let him have his way with the servant girls ! She concedes everything to him, she is willing to help him in every way he likes: it is the reparation she owes him. And thus the two of them, he in his incipient madness, she in a mood of grim despair, have recourse to the simple ideal of paganism, to joy, to the sun. "The sun!"—it is the last word of the play. In the soul of this proud Protestant there is a touch—however much transformed and disguised—of the feeling which drives the sailors of the North into some haunt of vice in the South. What is most singular about her is this, that in her anti-Christian return to nature—to immoral, reckless nature —she preserves her serene forehead, her sad lips, her grave Puritanical countenance. Her conscience is still to the fore. She is transgressing the rules of conduct with the same air and with the same deliberation with which she obeyed them until now. So essential is it to these good people of the North to have an explanation of life, to see a sense in it and a destined aim.

It would appear from this play, in which we see the asceticism of the North craving for the vacuous sensuality of the lands of the sun, that Ibsen sympathises with Fru Alving and with Oswald. But he tries to be fair and, as a contrast to Fru Alving, he depicts for us the excellent character who embodies the rules of life, Pastor Manders. The Pastor retains all the illusions and credulities, all the old regard for what is right. He has working with him the rascally old carpenter who legally is Regina's father and who is by way of being engaged in apostolic and benevolent activities. The Pastor is so touching in his rôle of continual dupe, that Fru Alving is quite moved by the sight of him. On one occasion, Engstrang having foisted on him some lie, he exclaims : " You see how careful one must be not to rash-judge our fellows. But how delightful it is to know one has been mistaken ! Don't you agree with me ? "

Fru Alving : I think you are a great big baby, Manders, and that you will always remain one !

The Pastor : I ?

Fru Alving (placing her two hands on his shoulders) : And I may add that I'm greatly tempted to throw my arms round your neck !

The Pastor (drawing back quickly) : No, no, God bless me ! What a strange fancy !

Fru Alving (smiling) : Oh, you needn't be so afraid of me !

THEATRICAL IMPRESSIONS

The Pastor : You have such an extraordinary way of expressing yourself sometimes !

The whole of this passage is delicious. And we also feel we might be tempted to kiss the fat, healthy cheeks of this " great big baby " of a pastor. This " great big baby," we have to note, is in his simple way a great sage. He suspects nobody, he does not know much about life or about men, and yet perhaps it is his serene ignorance which is right in the matter, as contrasted with the haughty and sophisticated bitterness of his friend. " Do you forget how miserable I was ? " Fru Alving asks him, and he replies : " The real spirit of revolt lies in looking for happiness in this life. What right have we to happiness ? No, we have to do our duty, Fru Alving."

The *joie de vivre* would be all very well if it rested only with ourselves to have a joyous life. But, supposing the Gospel of Thelema had been revealed twenty years earlier to Fru Alving and that, when she had betaken herself to the Pastor's, she had seduced him with her youth and beauty and had remained with him, it is very probable that her existence would not have been much happier, for while one may defy the law one cannot prevent it

from avenging itself. The cult of the joy of
living is practicable only when living is in fact
an easy matter. But this is so with few of us.
We cannot command happiness, and circumstances arise in which, joy and freedom from
care being in any case impossible, we recognise,
even without cherishing any definite faith at
all, that sacrifice and resignation are better
than revolt, if not to attain happiness, at least
to alleviate inevitable misery. And Fru Alving
herself will come to recognise this once more on
the morrow. She will no longer be a believer
but she will cease to rebel, and she will find
peace (possibly) in a state of detachment prouder
than that of rebellion. Thus we proceed,
according to events, from negation to faith or
to the desire for faith, or in the reverse direction.
Only, it is very seldom that our negation is
joyous. The naturalism of old was a delightful
thing because it was not a negation. It is sweet
to follow nature without thinking about it.
But one *cannot return to nature*, for the simple
reason that, in order to return to it, one must
have abandoned it, and, if we abandoned it,
that was because we could not keep to it. . . .
In fact, whether we are Christians or Pagans,
whether we submit or rebel, or whether we are

T

alternately in both camps in the course of this short life of ours, we do, alas, but as we have the force to do. We all of us, more or less, have our moral crises. That which is the theme of *Ghosts* is put before us with singular power and minuteness, and the soul we see suffering is stamped with the characteristics of a race notably different from our own. Hence the twofold interest of Ibsen's play.

[19th August, 1889. Vol. V.]

XXI

Chacun a sa Place. By A.-N. Ostrowsky.
Translated by E. Durand-Gréville.

THIS is the same Ostrowsky whose best-
known drama, *l'Orage*, was given last
winter at the Theâtre Beaumarchais.

Chacun à sa Place (or more correctly, *Ne
t'assieds pas dans le traîneau d'autrui*) dates from
1852. M. Durand-Gréville tells us in his interesting Preface that " the performances of this
exquisite and moving comedy have been almost
as numerous in Russia as those of *la Dame
blanche*." And, in truth, the theme of the piece,
very simple, very clear, very moral, very touching,
and with a happy ending, is one of those which,
when well handled, are surest to please the public.
A rich merchant has a daughter whom he wishes
to see married to a worthy youth of his own
world. She, however, is in love with a man of
rank who has spent all his money and who wants
to recoup himself with her *dot*. He carries her

off, hoping in this way to force her father's hand, but when he learns that the latter now consents to the marriage but refuses to part with a single sou of the *dot*, he reveals all that is worst in his character and the poor little goose, disillusioned, returns home. She finds awaiting her the good young fellow who had first sought her hand and who still loves her despite her escapade, and it is he whom she ends by marrying.

That is all. It is only a *berquinade*, but it is a Russian *berquinade*. Thus summarised, it is as mild as milk, but there is point and flavour in the developments of the action.

Roussakoff, the rich merchant, father of the girl, Avdotia, is a singularly living type. There is some resemblance between him, as regards both his character and the situation, and certain bourgeois characters in our French comedies— Chrysale, for instance, or, perhaps better still, Mme. Jourdain. Like Roussakoff, Mme. Jourdain is endowed with a gift of good, strong common sense ; she holds that everyone should keep his place, she distrusts all the fine words of Dorante ; like Roussakoff, she refuses her daughter to a man of rank, and is bent on marrying her to a man of her own walk in life. But note the different reasons for their conduct which are given us by the merchant of Théhéremouckine and the good woman of Paris. Mme. Jourdain is clear-sighted and practical : she is not humble. What she is most afraid of is the disdain of her son-in-law and the sharp remarks of her neighbours. You remember this excellent bit : " I don't want to have a son-in-law who will throw her parents in my daughter's face, and I don't want her to have children who will be ashamed to call me their grandmama. If they came visiting me in a grand carriage and pair, and if they weren't civil to someone round here, there'd be a lot of nasty talk about it. ' Look at Mme la Marquise, what a swell she is,' people would say. ' That's Mme. Jourdain's daughter—when she was a little girl she was satisfied to play with us at being ladies. She wasn't always so grand as she is now, and her grandparents sold cloth at the Porte-Saint-Innocent ! ' No, I don't want to listen to that kind of cackle. What I want is a young man who will be grateful to me for letting him have my daughter and to whom I can say : ' Sit you down there, my son, and have a snack with us ! ' "

In the reply of Roussakoff to Vikhoref, on the other hand, there is humility (perhaps just a little ironic) and the acceptance of caste. Moreover, there is more unselfishness in his attitude than in Mme. Jourdain's : Roussakoff ignores himself. He calculates not what the consequences of the marriage would be for him, but what they would be for his daughter. " Come, now, Excellency ! We are common folk, my daughter and I, we eat black bread. We are not the kind of people with whom your kind can ally themselves. All we are respected for is our money, and that's flat." So he urges ; and at another point : " It is just because I have her interests at heart that I won't give her to you. The idea that I should work her harm ! What sort of great lady would she make, do you imagine, a child like her, who has been shut up here between four walls and seen nothing of life ? Whereas she will make a good wife to a merchant, she will mind his house and look after her children." And again : " But no, you can't possibly love her. She's just a child, without education— she's not your sort. You have relatives and friends who would laugh at her as a simpleton, and you yourself would soon find her not to your taste. . . . Me land my daughter in such a position ! God forbid ! "

And there is another difference. Roussakoff, like all the characters in Russian plays, is a profoundly religious being. We may be quite certain that Chrysale or Mme. Jourdain, seeing Clitandre or Cléonte disappointed, would never think of saying to them : " You are feeling sad ? Cheer up, my boy ! You don't want to displease the good God, do you ? " Or else : " What strange things happen ! In the course of one's life one sees all kinds of things happening. If children do not respect their parents, if a woman does not live in peace with her husband, it is the doing of the devil. We must always be on our guard against him. There is much truth in the proverb : ' Don't be afraid of dying, but be afraid of sinning.' " Or : " My only anxiety at present is to establish my daughter properly. I should then have her happiness to contemplate and I should watch over my grandchildren, if God sent me any. . . . What else should I want beyond that ? I'd die in peace of mind. I'd know at least that there was someone left to have a Mass said for me and to speak well of me and keep me in mind."

I fancy that talk of this sort would have struck Molière as strangely ridiculous and " low class." Here is a strange thing to reflect upon. The France of the seventeenth century was still an entirely Christian country, both in faith and in practice ; everyone said his prayers, heard Mass and received the Sacraments ; those who lived bad lives did not for that reason lose their faith, and those who did lose their faith found it again regularly upon their death-bed. Religion, therefore, and the thoughts and preoccupations belonging to belief, ought to have been closely interwoven with the passions and actions of the men of that period in all classes. On the other hand, it is said, and is believed, that the comedies of Molière present an exact and sincere picture of this society. Now, there are assuredly no plays so absolutely devoid of religion and of religious feeling ; and, except in *Don Juan* and *Le Tartuffe*, in which piety is turned into ridicule, there is nothing, absolutely nothing, in all Molière's plays to indicate that the manners represented in them were those of a great Catholic country, firmly settled in its faith and strongly attached to the practices of its creed. Molière's work is, indeed, " laïcal " to a degree.

But we have to note further that the Tragedy of the seventeenth century was no more Christian than its Comedy, although Corneille and Racine, unlike Molière, were very good Christians. There is more of theology than of Christianity in *Polyeucte* ; the chief character of the drama is

a Christian, he is so in very exceptional conditions ; he has the fanaticism of the convert,
and his heroism is of a Roman or a Spanish
order. And as for the Christianity of Monime,
of Iphigénie, of Junie, or even of Phèdre—why
it is only a *façon de parler* : an absurdity of a
kind consecrated and sanctioned ever since
Châteaubriand's day, but, I am firmly convinced,
an absurdity none the less. I confess to you that
in its tone the theatre of our very Christian
seventeenth century has always seemed to me
to savour of the pre-Christian era.

The causes of this phenomenon I am not
qualified to give you. Are we to ascribe it
entirely to the great literary revolution—perhaps
pernicious—which is known as the Renaissance,
and which imposed on us the art-forms of a
civilisation two thousand years earlier than our
own, with the result that in our imaginative
works during the next two centuries we could
only express our souls circuitously and as it
were by trickery ? Or is it rather that in the
seventeenth century already, religion, for the
bulk of the population of France, had come to be
a thing just of external discipline and of inherited
tradition ? Or, rather, is it that the bourgeois
of those days (the normal subjects of the comedies)

were too good at heart, and had too much good taste, to suffer pious practices to be discussed in ordinary familiar conversation, after the fashion of the people of the thirteenth century or of the Russian *moujiks* of to-day? It would follow, would it not, that they would be shocked to have to listen in the theatre, in a place given up to profane amusement, to too direct an expression of their most intimate and most sacred feelings and of the most carefully-withheld part of their moral life? I confess I don't know what to say about it all.

What is certain is that Roussakoff is not a character out of Molière. This Russian has an inner life. When Avdotia insists that she wants to marry Vikhoref he does, indeed, reply at first : " Hold your tongue, you little fool ! You have heard my last word on the subject. You will marry Borodkine ! if you won't, then I shall have nothing more to say to you." But presently he recovers himself, and examines his conscience like the good Christian he is. " I have guarded you like the apple of my eye," he says to her : " I have been sinful on your behalf. I have given myself up to pride. . . . I have been so proud of you that I have not allowed other parents to talk to me about their children ; I believed there was no one better than you on earth. And now God is punishing me. I say to you, Avdotia—marry Borodkine! If you will not, you will not have my blessing. And don't let me hear any more talk of that worthless Vikhoref. I refuse to know him, do you hear me? Don't force me into sin!"

There is a pleasant little eighteenth century comedy in which the situation is almost the same as in *Chacun à sa Place*. It is *l'Ecole des Bourgeois*, by Dallainval. But how different the characters are!

Dallainval restricts to about thirty lines the rôle of Damis, the excellent youth who loves the heroine, Benjamine, and who forgives her after the Marquise de Moncade has revealed himself in his true character. No doubt the author regarded the part as an ungrateful one and uninteresting. Borodkine, the Damis of the Russian piece, keeps a grocer's shop and sells wine. He is good and simple-minded, with deep feelings. He speaks slowly and naïvely. We see him visiting the innkeeper Malomalsky, a friend of Avdotia's father, and he begins by making him drink a bottle of Lisbon wine. He says: " I have come, Sylvester Potapytch, to ask you something. . . . Wait until I have made my prayer to God." He gets up and bends forward his head.

Malomalsky : What is it you want me to do ?

Borodkine : Something connected with Maxim Fedotytch (Roussakoff). I want to ask you to put in a word for me.

Malomalsky : Something connected with . . . What can it be ?

Borodkine : It has to do with Avdotia Maximonna. . . . It would be my wish, and also my mother's wish——

Malomalsky : Why not ? It might be managed.

Borodkine : It seems to me that I want nothing at all in life except that Roussakoff should give me his daughter Avdotia, even with a penny.

Malomalsky : That can surely be managed.

Borodkine : Be my father and my benefactor ! Maxim Fedotytch will be coming to see you soon. Talk to him and I shall be indebted to you down to your dying day. That is to say, you will only have to say to me : " Ivan, do such and such a thing," and I shall do it with all my heart. . . . Would you like me to send for another bottle ?

Malomalsky : Good. Do so.

OSTROWSKY

Borodkine (to a waiter) : Send the boy round for another bottle.

In all these Russian dialogues there is a calm, a serenity, a kindliness which delight me. The speakers take their time, they are really talking to each other, they are not concerned to make effective repartees, they are unconscious of the existence of a theatrical " style," they do not seem to realise that they are upon a stage ; you cannot imagine anything less like a dialogue composed by M. Sardou—of whom, however, I wish to speak no ill ; finally, with all their awkwardnesses and diffusenesses, these Russian plays do somehow make us feel that we have real people living there before us. Their speech comes from afar—from the depths of the Steppes, in the first place, then from the depths of their naïve minds and from their hearts. And there is a great charm in it all.

This Borodkine is exquisitely portrayed ; he has about him the simplicity of the children of God. When Avdotia tells him that she loves Vikhoref, he turns his face to the window to weep for a moment ; then he takes his little guitar (we are in a land in which grocers play the guitar), chants a melancholy tune, beats his breast, kisses the young girl, and says to her : " Avdotia, remember how Ivan loved you ! "

In Dallainval's slight comedy, poor Damis wins eventually his little minx of a Benjamine, but it is manifest that he would have cleared off if Benjamine had previously eloped with Moncade. The knowing young Frenchman (he is to be pitied) would not run the risk of looking ridiculous. Now, when Borodkine meets Avdotia for the first time after she has parted from Vikhoref and returned home, he says to her : " Mademoiselle Avdotia, as this gentleman, owing to his low behaviour, no longer merits your love, I may have a little hope ? " And later : " What does it matter to me if ill be spoken ? I love Avdotia and I don't mind about all that." Note, that at this moment, if he is sure of Avdotia's repentance and suffering, he does not know, after all, what has happened between her and the handsome officer. But he loves her. And there is something else : " Avdotia," he says to her, " do you think, then, that I have no feelings in me ? I am not a wild beast. I have in me a spark of God." And that is why he says to her father : " Give her to me. I will take her." And he becomes angry : " You promised her to me this morning. I do not take back my word, and you, do you take back yours ? That is not right, Monsieur Roussakoff ! She is your daughter. I do not deny that ; but that is no reason why you should do her harm. Mlle. Avdotia has had quite enough trouble already—someone has got to take her part. A wrong has been done her, and it is she who is being blamed. In our home, at any rate, she will have my mother and me to say kind words to her. What does it all amount to in the end ? Are we not all sinners ? Is it for us to judge ? "

And Avdotia ? Listen to Benjamine's alert chatter in *l'Ecole des Bourgeois* : " . . . I am more impatient than you, mother ; for, besides the pleasure of seeing myself the wife of a *grand seigneur*, the fact is that, owing to the way this affair has gone while Damis has been away in the country, I shall be glad to be actually married when he comes back so as to escape his reproaches. . . . Long live the Marquis de Moncade ! " Poor Avdotia is not thinking of the pleasure of seeing herself " the wife of a *grand seigneur*." " I don't know how I came to love him," she declares. " I can't explain it to myself. . . . I met him at Anna Antonovna's. . . . I was having tea there when I saw him come in. . . . He was so handsome. . . . I felt my heart beating and I said to myself : ' This will mean unhappiness for me.' '' And whereas Benjamine is as lively as she can be, Avdotia '' remains in a corner all day long like a woman condemned to death ; nothing gives her any pleasure ; she doesn't want to see anybody.'' Benjamine hides herself from her former lover, but it is to Borodkine himself that Avdotia makes her confession. Like all the passionate characters in the Russian drama, she is '' possessed.'' With her pale-yellow hair and blue eyes full of that infinite sweetness to be seen in Russian eyes, what she has in her heart is that deep love to which there is no resistance. She faints when her father refuses her to the man she loves ; she follows her victor weeping, knowing well that she does wrong. But she follows him. And when he rejects her, when he lets her see the brutality of his soul, she recovers herself with the same sudden violence with which she abandoned herself. . . . And this, as you know, is eminently Russian. A Russian will watch himself sinning half his life and the other half he will be publicly confessing his sin. Avdotia recalls Catherine in *l'Orage* a little. Do you remember her ? And Borodkine is reminiscent a little of Robanoff, Catherine's husband. They have very little complexity

about them, and yet they are profound. Coming
of a race which is still young and almost unspoilt,
they have passions of extreme force—all the
more that, with their mystical way of looking
at things, they view these passions as the effect
of some mysterious power, and this notion of
fatality intensifies them. And their virtues,
also, possess a kind of silent energy ; their
constant preoccupation with the other world and
with sin, combined with the influence of solitude
and of the limitless expanses in which they live,
communicate to all their feelings a religious
gravity, an accent of sincerity and certainty not
to be met with elsewhere. It would seem that
these *moujiks* and tradesmen, so ignorant and
so serious, live morally almost the same lives as
our early mediæval ancestors. Those ancestors
of ours, however, had only weakling poetasters
to express their soul, men scarcely more intelligent than themselves, superficial observers, possessed of little verve and writing in a style which
was hard and dry ; whereas we have great poets
and great psychologists to interpret to us the
Christian simplicity and the depth of passion in
the lives of the peasants of Russia.

The other characters in *Chacun à sa Place* are
almost negligible. It would seem that in Russia

U

the wicked and the absurd are all quite crude
and without shades in their character. Vikhoref,
the ex-officer, displays such brutality and folly
and cynicism, one wonders that little Avdotia
could possibly have loved him. There is an old
maid, too, Arina, sister to Roussakoff, romantic
and affected, who is merely a facile caricature.
I prefer the worthy innkeeper, Malomalsky. In
France, in our drama of to-day, an innkeeper is
always a big fat jovial man and a babbler. Now,
this good Malomalsky is as grave as a stork and
can't put two sentences together. The truth is
that there may be innkeepers who do not talk
too much, and it is also the truth that in the
smallest details of their work we may find in
the Russians a greater sincerity or simplicity than
we ourselves possess.

[Sept., 1889. Vol. V.]

XXII

At the "Chat Noir" and Elsewhere

Most of the volumes of *Impressions* include some shorter pieces devoted to what may be called the side-shows of theatrical Paris. Jules Lemaître delighted in them. He is often at his best when discoursing upon some popular performance at the Alcazar d'Eté, some eccentric novelty in a cabaret of Montmartre, some fairy-play or ballet or *revue*. In these little articles, however, he is apt to be even more difficult to translate than in his ordinary *critiques*. I shall venture on only a very few examples—enough merely to give a notion of their scope and variety. Here, to begin with, is a note-worthy tribute to the genius of Caran d'Ache, as exemplified in a shadowgraph at the famous little Théâtre du Chat Noir :

CARAN D'ACHE'S *Epopée* is, in effect, an epic poem without words and in thirty scenes, the characters in which are *ombres chinoises* : it is a representation of the great epic of Napoleon—the battle of Austerlitz, the retreat from Russia, the apotheosis of the Emperor, the return of the troops to Paris. The big events are made to alternate with comic episodes : we see the Emperor going out of his tent, followed by a poodle, and passing a sentinel

who presents arms; we see the captive kings,
lean or corpulent, with their royal trappings,
crowns or sceptres, in their hands; the hero-
worshipping populace in " costumes of the period,"
climbing upon ladders or perched on great wine-
casks to see the army on the march; the pre-
sumptuous individual who pushes forward too
eagerly and who is brought up sharp by a
grenadier; and so on, and so on. The effect of
the funny scenes was easy to imagine in advance,
but what one could not foresee so well was that
these little silhouettes, cut out in zinc and set
moving behind a white cloth little more than a
yard in width, could communicate to us a touch
of the spirit of war and of the sense of grandeur.
And yet so it was. The picture of the review,
that of the battle, that of the retreat, and others
as well, are of real beauty—I had almost said, of
solemn beauty. When one comes to reflect upon
it, this is explicable enough. M. Caran d'Ache,
whose hand is very bold and very sure, contrives
to give us the illusion of life from the start by
the convincing truth of his simplified little outlines. He has resort not to caricature but
rather to a peculiar method of draughtsmanship
which—the depicting of faces lying outside its
scope—so handles bodies as to intensify their

individuality and expressiveness. With a few strokes, he gives us eyeless, mouthless beings, who yet are all life and movement : types which, by the cut of their limbs, the carriage of their heads, their *empanachement*, their dash and go, can only be heroes of the *grande armée*. We recognise, instantly, the profile of *l'Homme à l'oreille cassée*. . . . But that is not all : this kind of drawing, by means of its very limitations, is admirably fitted for the rendering of the life of crowds—of that life in common in which the individual lives are merged. M. Caran d'Ache knows this well. By the exactness of the perspective which he preserves in his long lines of soldiers, he conveys to us the illusion of numbers, immense numbers, indefinite numbers. By the automatic movement which sets them all advancing simultaneously, he conveys to us the illusion of a single mind, a single thought, animating countless men, and, consequently, the idea of a power immeasurable. . . . And then, of course, we all have our minds full of those great wars and of the extraordinary mortal who worked us so much harm, but who brought us so much glory ; and we ourselves sink back into the mass of our race as we gaze at his legendary figure, half heroic, half grotesque, dominating the fields of blood wherein History mysteriously takes shape. . . . We smiled the other evening, but we experienced, also, something very like emotion. That was a real triumph for Caran d'Ache, and one well earned. His mute poem, with the flitting shadow-shapes, is, I think, the only epic that we have in our literature.

The above appeared on January 3, 1887, and is included in Volume II of the *Impressions*. What follows, dated 28 August, 1888, is the beginning of an account of two productions of the *Enfant Prodigue* order at the Cercle Funambulesque, and is to be found in Volume III :

Ah ! How I wish I were a Pierrot-Critic !

" But that is what you are ! " you will retort wickedly.

I must explain. What I wish is that I might express myself upon the subject of these new pantomimes through the medium merely of attitudes, gestures and grimaces—that I might silently mime this feuilleton instead of having to write it. How much more quickly I could get it done, and how much clearer and more vivid it would be ! My eyes fixed, all my features tense, shuddering a little at moments, and yet with a flame of ecstasy in my eyes, I would give you all the indications of that *douce terreur* and that *pitié charmante* of which Boileau speaks.

AT THE " CHAT NOIR "

Then I would strike my two hands one against the other for several seconds ; next, raising my eyebrows, I would shake my head slowly four or five times in quick succession ; finally, I would shape my lips into a great round *O* and protrude them, and, lifting to them the outstretched fingers of my right hand, I would despatch from them a swift, resonant kiss. And you would understand at once that *Colombine Pardonnée* had pleased me much and had inspired me with great admiration. After which, I would withdraw into myself, I would half close my eyes, I would place one hand against my brow, I would remain for some time motionless. And you would con- clude immediately that I was lost in thought, that the pleasure I felt was amazing me and embarrassing me, that I was seeking to analyse it in my own mind, that I was putting to myself, on the subject of this *Colombine Pardonnée*, ques- tions subtle and deep which I was finding it difficult to answer. And so, too, with *l'Amour de l'Art :* to tell you what I thought of it, I would first smile artfully (at least, I would endeavour to do so), then laugh my great, mute laugh. After which, I would repeat the above performance—the display of admiration, the head-shaking, the kiss, the reverie—the reverie a little less prolonged. . . . But, alas! You might find it all inadequate! . . .

And so he must be content to describe in words two very exquisite dramas, which proved beyond all refutation that words were vanities!

It is remarkable how little space is given in the *Impressions* to the players as compared with the plays. Jules Lemaître concedes very few of his pages to the outstanding figures of the Paris theatre—to Sarah Bernhardt and Mme. Réjane, Mounet-Sully and the Coquelins; to Mme. Yvette Guilbert, we find only a few casual allusions. An exception is made in favour of that *rose d'automne* Mme. Anna Judic, on her reappearance at the Eldorado Music Hall on October 8, 1893. She gets an entire *impression* to herself.

Mme. Judic's charms—Lemaître assures us, are unfaded. Her face is still exquisite, its expression, as ever, " *si gentille et si douce* "; and he reminds us of the things wherein she excels—*nuances*, *sous-entendus*, words softly murmured, " the while her eyes are all innocence and her lips all knowingness." "She is, in truth, a combination of impudicity and propriety "; " yes, she combines the two—by what mystery I cannot explain."

He gives us next a delicately-phrased *résumé* of two of her best-known songs, *Ne me chatouillez pas*! and *La Mousse*. The first is in four stanzas, now sentimental, now suggestive, now broadly comic. It ends with the emotion of a lady who is suspected of concealing contraband goods about her person, *et dont les vêtements sont explorés par la main impersonelle de notre douane nationale*. The second—with pretty and even poetical touches in it—is so extremely daring in one passage that Lemaître, *n'ayant pas la plume dont se servait un jour Théophile Gautier pour exprimer un de ses plus vifs regrets esthétiques*, has to refrain from indicating to us its burden with more precision. That he himself laughed at it, he does not deny!

But " *Interroges-toi quand tu ris!* " was a maxim which Jules Lemaître always practised—it might almost have been a maxim of his own devising. Accordingly, he proceeds to ask himself what is to be said about the fair Anna and her *libertinage élégant* from the standpoint of ethics. In some moods, his answer to the question might be more severe, but to-night he is at his most benignant. To-night, he is inclined to view such matters in the spirit of that smiling Buddhist, · M. Anatole France.* All things considered, he refuses to frown. The ways of the world have to be accepted, and as, to all seeming, some measure of sexual immorality is an essential ingredient in " urban diversions," better Mme. Judic's methods than most others. As we are bound to have vice and folly, let us have them at least without ugliness. . . . Jules Lemaître is tolerant, we may admit, in good company. Did not Edmund Burke—*his* eyes, also, on the French capital—say very much the same thing just a hundred years before ?

Here, finally, is an *impression* of quite a different order, one from the Folies-Bergère :

My fellow-men having allowed me a respite from their affairs this week, I shall talk to you about our sisters the beasts, as Saint Francis of Assisi used to say.

Boney, the little Folies-Bergère absurdity, is, beyond question, the most sympathetic elephant

* There is no reference in Jules Lemaître's text just here to M. France, but the two men, friends and mutual admirers, always recognised the essential similarity of their attitude towards life. Not long before, Lemaître had classed himself with Anatole France as one of a group of French writers apt to indulge in *cette voluptueuse curiosité intellectuelle*, which M. Paul Desjardins, in a lecture, had been pointing to as characteristic of the Buddhists of Paris. (See *Impressions de Theâtre*, Vol. VI.)

THEATRICAL IMPRESSIONS

I have ever met in my already long career as a circus-goer. He is an infant—he is only about as big as a very big ox. What a happy temperament is his, and what vivácity of mind! His entire physiognomy speaks of gentle roguishness. A small, pointed clown's cap is fixed upon the summit of his brow like a rock emerging from the sea. A huge loose garment, of variegated and brilliant colours, envelops him down to the knees. Boney, it is obvious, relishes this disguise. He is agreeably conscious of looking comic. The pleasure he takes in being gazed at sparkles in his small eyes.

Having described some of Boney's achievements and accomplishments in the ring and the air of gaiety which seemed common to him and the other elephants taking part in the performance, Lemaître proceeds to speculate as to whether they were all as happy as they looked. Perhaps, really, their lot was not as enviable as that of their brothers in liberty, roaming over the great plains and in and out of the great forests; he remembers " those romantic elephants of Châteaubriand, who could say their morning prayers beneath the boundless heavens and with their trunks offer incense to the rising sun "; and, he feels for a moment, that it must be unpleasant for such enormous brutes to be pent up in small stables and not to be allowed even to stroll along the Boulevards. Presently, another aspect of the matter occurs to him:

But no: on thinking it over, I have come to the conclusion that their fate, in spite of all, is an enviable one. If you except the deer, and also certain domestic animals which we overwork, it appears to me that the creatures which have most real happiness* are those which live most with man and which have penetrated farthest into intimacy with him (I may add, for the benefit of frivolous persons, that I am not now talking about insects). The animals which we honour with our friendship are, I say, the happiest, because they have discovered for themselves the purpose of life, a purpose which is above themselves and beyond which evidently their dreams cannot soar.

Our own misfortune is that we are the most perfect race inhabiting the planet. Therefore, we cannot live for anything above ourselves and we have to concentrate upon our own aspirations. Hence, our unappeasable disquietude. If there were upon earth another living species as superior to us as we are to our good dogs and our good elephants, what would not be our comfort and our joy! To draw near to this species, to obey it, love it, serve it, to try to understand it—that would be for us the manifest end and aim of our existence ; we should be

* Lemaître writes " *les plus heureuses moralement,*" but the word " *moralement* ", like " *moral* " very often, cannot be quite literally translated into English.

unable to conceive of a greater happiness, of a greater honour, and we should not even think of seeking anything beyond.

This is exactly the state of mind of the worthy animals which live by our side. What can be more touching than their submission, their trust, their goodwill, their unceasing efforts to lift themselves up to our level and to live, in so far as possible, within our life ? And how well they know how to love us ! The most impassioned biped of us all will never attain to the degree of absolute devotion that is shown by some poor poodle towards its master, by some little griffon towards its dame.

THE END